I0181010

The Lonely Place
Re-Visioning Adolescence
and the Rite of Passage

A Cultural Guide
to Strengthening our Youth

Patricia Jamie Lee, M.A.

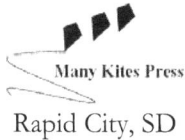

Many Kites Press

Rapid City, SD

Many Kites Press
Copyright © 2010 Patricia Jamie Lee

All rights reserved. No part of this book may be reproduced or transmitted in any form or by any means, electronic or mechanical, including photo-copying, recording or by any information storage and retrieval system with-out written permission from the author, except for the inclusion of brief quotations.

Many Kites Press
3907 Minnekahta Dr.
Rapid City, SD 57702
www.manykites.com

ISBN 978-0-9618469-5-4

High schools, colleges, universities and reading groups may want to purchase this book wholesale to generate discussions on adolescence and rites of passage. For wholesale or discount information call 1-800-486-8940.

Printed in the United States

What others are saying about The Lonely Place

Once in a long while a book comes along that tells us something new and important about the society in which we live. Jamie Lee's book on rites of passage (and the lack of them) in western society today is in this class. It gives us a new tool with which to see ourselves and our culture. Using her deep comprehension of American Indian culture as a baseline, she brings a new clarity to the mainstream culture. Lucid and exciting to read, it clarifies important aspects of who and what we are today, and gives us clues to what we may yet become. ~Dr. Lawrence LeShan (author of The Psychology of War, Cancer as a Turning Point) NY, NY)

The "Generation Gap" has existed in Western Culture for many years, indeed for many centuries, but is more acute than ever in the 21ˢᵗ century. Patricia Jamie Lee describes how bright-eyed babies often turn into sullen teenagers. More important, she tells her readers what can be done about it. By reviewing the rituals used by Native peoples, and by revisiting their wisdom, she presents practical approaches that harness the power of love, and evoke challenges that empower rather than overwhelm today's youth, too many of whom are falling through the cracks of a culture that is badly torn and in need of mending. ~Krippner, PhD (Co-editor, The Psychological Impact of War Trauma On Civilians.) Saybrook Inst., SF, CA

This book is very helpful in probing the perils and problems and joys of adolescence in a toxic society, and I heartily recommend it to those who care about our youth. ~Stephen R. Sroka, Ph.D., President, Health Education Consultants, Adjunct Asst. Prof., Case Western Reserve University

Other Books by Patricia Jamie Lee

Washaka—The Bear Dreamer, a novel

Feeling Good About Feeling Bad, nonfiction

The Taming Power of Love,
A Handbook of Family Constellation Work, nonfiction

Albert's Manuscript, a visionary novel,

Coming in 2010

One Drum, a visionary novel

Silver, a visionary novel

To read excerpts and short works visit
Jamie Lee's blog at www.jamielee.manykites.org

Table of Contents

Introduction

For the past several years I've been haunted by a young fourteen-year-old girl I never met. Gina Score died in a boot camp training school in Plankinton, SD[1]. Her family, from a small eastern South Dakota town, was like many families from the Midwest. Generally, we live simple lives here, but Gina somehow got off on the wrong foot—like others of us did at her age. She did some shoplifting, skipped school, and got herself into trouble with the police. In July of 1999, she was put in the boot camp in an attempt to 'shape her up' and get her back on the right track. Fashioned after the model of military training, boot camp for teens is not summer camp.

Five days after Gina arrived in Plankinton the girls from Cottage B, fifteen of them in all, went on an early morning run down a road outside the complex. Both the temperature and the humidity were about seventy. Gina, weighing over two hundred pounds, couldn't complete the run. When she collapsed, the staff counselors thought she was faking it and let her lie there in the sun—for three hours. Eyewitnesses reported that Gina roused herself once, tried to make it the last 100 feet to her cottage, but collapsed again. Her skin was pale, her lips blue, and she had urinated on herself. Still, the staff did nothing.

When the paramedics were called at last, Gina was taken by ambulance to the hospital, but on the way her heart gave out. Paramedics tried to revive her but the damage was too severe—her internal body temperature had topped the thermometer at 108 degrees.

This will be the most depressing and devastating story I'll tell here because Gina's story is the reason I finally finished this book. I can't get her off my mind. After researching kids and culture for over ten years, it was Gina who finally pushed me out of analysis and into action.

Our children suffer. A shocking five million plus have been diagnosed as ADD or ADHD and placed on Ritalin[2]. Suicide is now the third most common cause of death for young people[3]. Two hundred thousand young people are incarcerated each year, with 84,000 of them placed in solitary confinement for twenty-four hours or more[4].

There is, of course, no easy answer to the challenges our current culture presents to its young. We can't simply pack a bag and send them off to seek their fortune. Something much more complex is required.

As I began writing this book, I found myself grappling with fundamental questions sweetly reminiscent of my own youth. Why am I here? What have I come to do? Do I have the right or the duty to decide for anyone what is best for them—even my own children? Is it possible to be guide, mentor and eventually Elder to those who now travel the paths I walked earlier? What are the golden links between mind, body, spirit, family, and culture?

It's as if in searching for the right initiation for my growing children I was, myself, initiated.

This is not just a book but the *story* of a book which took me over ten years to write. The journey has not been an easy one. It seems we are training our young people to be violent, alone, and dead to the world. They are in the lonely place. From early childhood on our children face a barrage of violent images on television, video games, and the internet. They watch ridiculous programs where the children act big, the parents act stupid and the whole family is clueless. They attend schools where earnest educators attempt to stuff information into their brains without thought of the natural human learning process.

Growing children into conscious, healthy adults is a web which connects to all aspects of our current culture. There are no easy answers. This effort, I hope, will be part of a long, honest cultural conversation about what we need to do to ensure a healthy future for our young people.

The messages of this book will seem confusing or contradictory at times. They will push against the tidal wave of negative energy flowing out toward our young. They will examine the tendency toward pathological diagnoses and the criminalization of the adolescent—as if being a teen were a sickness or a crime. They will challenge us to search our own development for signs of the uninitiated adult within.

I will also contradict myself by suggesting first that we do as the Lakota mothers do for their littlest ones— call them *dear*, *sweet* and *precious one* to pull their little spirits tightly to us. Then I'll tell suggest that with our teens we must push them hard with strong tests and challenges. And finally, for those on the edge of adulthood, I suggest we bless them—and then get out of their way and stop doing for them what they should be doing for themselves.

Throughout these chapters I will wander through the many fields of science, medicine, psychology, and spiritual thought. At one point I will venture into the Family constellation of the German psychotherapist, Bert Hellinger.[5] At another point, I will build a map that orients us to the higher levels of development. The desired end result of all of these seemingly varied topics is to build and strengthen the cultural cradle that contains the child and his family and our culture.

In the chapters to follow there are many references to the public radio series my husband, Milt, and I produced called *Oyate Ta Olowan—The Songs of the People*.[6] This series consists of fifty-two public radio documentary programs on Native American music and stories. Over five years we traveled deeply into Indian country to meet and interview The *Oyate*, which means "The People" in Lakota. This incredible journey taught me much, and I gratefully acknowledge all the Elders and teachers who have contributed to the information presented here.

I would like to dedicate this book to my three children, Nichol, Lisa, and Thomas who have taught me so much about becoming a human being. Without you guys, my life would have been a desert.

Chapter 1
Through The Tipi to the Rising Sun

On a slope of Bear Butte, a gentle mountain in South Dakota, a young man awaits the vision that will organize and guide his life. For four days he will fast, pray, and sleep alone under the night sky. At the base of the mountain, his family and friends wait for him.

On a sandy stretch of land in Arizona just north and east of Phoenix, a young woman dressed in white buckskin wears an abalone shell like a crown on her forehead and carries a crooked staff. For four days she chants, prays, and dances as her family and friends gather around to support her.

On a beach in northern Minnesota, a young woman takes a dare and drinks a quart of Southern Comfort. She nearly dies. In the emergency room, her family and friends wipe tears and pray—that she will live through the night.

On a street in Los Angeles, a young man takes a gun and shoots a rival gang member. His buddies accept him, but two families gather now—one for a trial, one for a funeral.

As unlikely as it sounds, there is a common denominator here. All four young people are performing a ritual, or a rite of passage, that has developed in the culture that surrounds them. All four have responded to something deep within themselves that says there *must* be a passage from childhood to adulthood. The difference is that the young man on the mountain and the young woman in white buckskin were raised in a culture that recognizes— and prepares itself—for this powerful event.

11

The need is real. It captures us all, sending us through a second birth canal toward the makings of soul that gives our life meaning. I still remember that gnawing feeling of restless desire, wanting answers, and pushing against constraint. As young people, we walked lonely roads or beaches staring out at starry night skies and wondering what . . . what . . . does it all mean? What have I come here to do? We found all of our boundaries and then tested them. We forced our parents to lie awake far into the night wondering and praying that we would make it home . . . this time.

It happened to all of us, but somewhere along the historical trail, the massive, brilliant energy of adolescence became something to fear and dread rather than to nurture and guide. Society began the nasty game of passing the buck; the church should take care of it, the family, the schools, and the politicians . . . no . . . it's up to the law. And while we quibbled and blamed, our children stopped becoming young men and women and became *teenagers.*

This topic was of special interest to me not just as an educator and scholar, but also as a parent. When I first began this book, my three children were moving toward adulthood. I was consumed with the question of "What do they need?" in order to make a strong passage from my home to one of their own making.

During the recording of the *Oyate* series, we had the opportunity to attend an Apache Sunrise Ceremony[1] performed as an initiation ritual for a young girl. This beautiful and complex rite of passage ceremony is filled with small, intricate pieces of which I can only give you my experience as an outsider to that culture.

We arrived at the ceremonial grounds just outside of Ft. McDowell, Arizona at sunrise on the second day of the ceremony. The young girl being initiated was dressed in a beautiful white buckskin dress and tall moccasins with a piece of gleaming abalone adorning her forehead.

She looked ageless, a portrait drawn into the lost pages of some beautiful storybook. Family members, mostly women, surrounded her. The sandy, desert ceremonial grounds were filled with her community—there to share her experience and to support her through it.

The ceremony went on day and night with a dozen or more male singers chanting endless repetitive melodies that stir the blood and awaken the senses. At night, a huge bonfire was built. Mysterious crown dancers came out dressed in dark regalia and wearing tall, elaborate crowns. It is said that the crown dancers take on the spirits of the surrounding mountains during the ceremony, and when it's over, the crowns are hidden in the mountains and never used again. Throughout the long days of dancing, the girl carries a crooked staff with a feather dangling from it. As she steps the endless beat, she pounds the staff on the earth.

I watch, wondering if she is tired, how long has she danced . . . can she go on? I also wonder what private things her aunties and grandmothers have told her about becoming a woman. It is said that during the time of the ceremony, the young girl becomes a healer. Members of the tribe bring their babies and their ill Elderly family members to be healed by her.

During the ceremony I can see the girl is transformed by this whole experience. She is no longer a girl—and certainly not a teenager or an adolescent—but someone else. Her eyes appear to see far beyond the ceremonial grounds and the people around her.

Toward the end of the ceremony, the girl is placed on her knees facing the sun. An aunt, her mentor, supports her from behind as the girl dances from her knees, raising her hands again and again towards the sky. At last, the Medicine Man brings out a basket of corn pollen paint and a brush, and paints her face and head with this thin yellowish mud. I watch and am transfixed. As the mud dries, she looks ancient, timeless— as if carved on a sandstone wall and left there for eternity. When the painting is completed, the Medicine Man turns to the crowd and flicks the loaded brush into the crowd until we, too, are painted.

This astounding ceremony has only one purpose—to assist that young girl into her maturity, to guide her in the passage from girl to woman. The weeks of planning, the tremendous expense of feeding the crowds and preparing for the ceremony are all taken on by her family in order that she may have this important experience of the soul.

I was touched to the core by this ceremony. Deep in my heart I longed to offer such a transformation to my own daughters—or to myself. I realized that I was grieving for the young girl in me still awaiting such an event. I wanted feathers and visions and long dark nights in a tipi under a wide, black sky. I was also grieving for the parent in me who wanted heavenly creatures to dance out of the dark and speak to my children in mysterious languages that only he or she would understand. I wanted the mysteries of the universe to unfold their secrets for my children so that they might suffer less from this human condition than I have.

When comparing this beautiful ceremony to my own passage, I found, sadly, that there was no comparison. For me, womanhood brought only an unexplained feeling of shame. Beginning menstruation was a fearful time, and growing breasts brought only disrespect, sexual innuendo, teasing, and crass new words like "boobs" and "tits." In sixth and seventh grade, we had a gym teacher who would not allow a menstruating girl to swim. She sent us to an open study hall filled with taunting boys who knew exactly why we were there. There was no honor in that moment.

After attending the Sunrise Ceremony, I felt robbed, ripped off by a culture that couldn't see me at that age. I also walked away from that night determined to discover ways to strengthen the cultural cradle so that my children, and their children, could experience this important transition like the young Apache girl stepping through the tipi to the rising sun.

In addition to the Sunrise Ceremony, our extensive travels into Indian Country gave my husband and me the chance to see what many native people are still doing for their young—rituals and ceremonies with no equivalent in the melting pot of mainstream America. We watched dedicated Hopi girls and boys learn the Butterfly dance. We stood under a star-studded sky on the northern coast of California watching a young Hupa girl perform her first ceremonial dance dressed in buckskin stitched heavily with glowing white shells. We attended small community powwows and watched the young native boys and girls shed their baggy jeans and T-shirts and adorn themselves with the fine regalia of their ancestors.

When I compare all this to the little that we in mainstream America have to offer, it nearly makes me weep. Our culture and, sadly, many remaining indigenous cultures, are no longer connected to their tribal ways. What remains of our rite of passage rituals have been badly diluted, reduced to such minor markers as getting a driver's license, going to prom, getting a diploma, etc.

Today, our culture is riddled with the shards and pieces of initiation rituals. I view these remnants as an archeologist might view an old city buried beneath a windswept, sandy plain. There, in the humps and bumps that remain, is the record of what was once a living, active civilization.

Exploring the way a youth emerges out of childhood to take his or her rightful place as an adult in the community is not a simple task. It forces us to examine both modern and ancient ways of being, to evaluate and determine what is important—and what is simply flotsam. It also forces us, as adults, to look into the hidden corners of our own development.

As a culture, instead of honoring and teaching our youth, we have fallen into the bad habit of shunning and discounting the vibrant and sometimes aching needs young people have. Adolescence is not an aberration, not just a loud squawk on the human behavior scale but a potent and sometimes agonizing leap toward adulthood. It is an event that crosses all cultural boundaries from country to country, race to race, and past to present. Making this leap requires every ounce of courage and strength we can muster. Michael Ventura (1994),[2] a provocative therapist and writer, said of our society:

> They fail to understand that a psychic structure that has remained constant for 100,000 years is not likely to be altered in a generation by stimuli that play upon its surfaces. What's really going on is very different. The same, raw, ancient content is surging through youth's psyches, but adult culture over the last few centuries has forgotten how to meet, guide, and be replenished by its force.

If the event itself (adolescence) remains unchanged throughout history, then the problems exploding in our young people must come from the way that we greet the event. We won't erase adolescence by ignoring it or by dismissing it. We must meet it head on. Not only that, we must meet it with great respect and love.

During the early stages of research into this project, I had my seventeen-year-old daughter take a tape deck to her high school and ask her classmates, "What do you think adults think of you?" The responses were shocking. "They think we're losers. Nothing. Worse than nothing. They think we are worthless." One young man said that when he walks down the street, adults sometimes cross the street to avoid meeting him head on.

Ventura (1994) said:

> When we don't have apt words for something, it's because of an unspoken collective demand to avoid thinking about it. That's how scary 'adolescence' is. Which is also to say, that's how scary our very own unspeakable adolescence was . . . What we cannot face when we cannot face the young is, plainly, ourselves.

Are we afraid to face our own undeveloped, uninitiated adolescent selves? How many of us are still caught in the cusp between childhood and adulthood, unable to fully make the crossing, stopped by fear, unpolished understanding, and selfish, childish desires? It would explain the current dilemma. Ventura reminded us that, "Tribal adults didn't run from this moment in their children as we do; they celebrated it. They would assault their adolescents with, quite literally, holy terror; rituals that had been kept secret from the young till that moment. . . ."

Fascinated by what Ventura said about *assaulting our young*, I thought of the students at the high school my children attended. They drive around in their SUV's and new Hondas wearing designer clothes and carrying cell phones. This image and the word "assault" clearly don't line up.

During this same time I also spoke with several classes of juniors and seniors at the local high school. After some discussion of rites of passage, I asked them outright, "Suppose I gave you a task that was so difficult and so challenging that, when you had completed it, you would know *without a doubt* that you had been completely transformed. How many of you would take the challenge?" Their hands shot into the air. It still raises the hair on my arms to recall that energy. These kids want—no, need—the defining, transformative experience.

The critical question here is how can we create what we did not experience and can no longer recall from our own cultural roots? This question stopped me cold for many years. In America our roots are sometimes shallow or even broken. Ancient rite of passage rituals arise from a deeply rooted traditional culture, and many of us have lost that connection.

Can we recreate what has been lost? And what would a modern day rite of passage ritual look like? How would it take place?

The Cradle of Culture

Culture is a multifaceted word. For some it means such things as art, literature, and theater. For others it means the social structures and morals that bind us, and for still others it is ethnic, tied to our ancestral roots. For most of us, however, our culture is unclear and blurred, like a watercolor painting on which a glass of water has been spilled. If we are to explore, with any effectiveness, the re-building of a strong culture that knows how to respond to its young, we must know first of which we speak. Culture, community, society—what do all these words mean?

In Chevak, Alaska, there is a small Chup'ik village planted up near the Bering Sea that is accessible only by small plane. On a collection trip for *Oyate*, we stayed in the home economics room of the local school, sleeping on nap mats and cooking our packaged food on one of the many available stovetops. The village children, young and old, followed us at every turn, drilling us about who we were, and what we were doing there. Their trust and openness was astounding. I yearned to know what right combination of community gave them such faith that the world was a good and safe place.

The first evening several of the young teens were preparing to perform a traditional dance at the Alaskan Federation of Natives in Anchorage. We joined the Elders and community members watching them dance. The boys wore white *chuspic* smocks and jeans, and the girls had on calico *chuspics* and headpieces trimmed with caribou fur. It was amazing to watch them dance with precise, disciplined moves to the loud thrumming of four wide-rimmed drums. It was graceful, beautiful . . . peaceful.

The image that stayed with me most strongly, however, was the row of Elders against the far wall, all there to train and teach the young people. There was something so right in that image; the young under direct tutelage of the Elders. At the end of the line of Elderly men hitting the drum was a single young drummer following their moves.

A few nights later I lay awake in a hotel in Anchorage thinking about this book on adolescent rites of passage. Oddly, I found myself jealous of the *Chupiks*, the *Inuits*, the *Athabascans*, the *Lakotas*—so many indigenous people who, in spite of the ravages of the past 500 years, still hold fast to a culture that includes far more than the language and music. They have a sense of identity that stretches back thousands of years. They have their Elders lined up against the wall watching them dance and sing. I thought about my own mixed-blood background and realized that all that remains of my original culture is the knowledge of how to make *lefse*. There are no Elders, no rituals, no safe borders to define who I am, and no cultural memory beyond my own generation. Rather, I'm liquefied in the great melting pot that is rapidly reaching melt down. I am an American.

Most Americans of European decent are several centuries away from their own indigenous, tribal cultures. There is no memory of the rites and rituals that may have been practiced in small German, Norwegian, or Irish

19

villages, no knowledge of ancestral stories, and no recollection of the mysticism or songs that led their own ancestors into maturity with a sense of identity and connection. With the great migration from Europe to America, often driven by famine, hardship and war, the ancestral, indigenous cultures that were perhaps thousands of years old were shattered as the masses boarded those ships and left their homelands. This is true also for many who left or were forced from their homelands in Africa, Spain, Asia, and on and on.

Only a few American ethnic cultures still have Elder-based initiation and rituals to support the young person in his or her passage into adulthood. My Internet searches uncovered many movements within the African-American, Latino and Native American cultures to return to the use of these ancient rituals of initiation for the young. I celebrate these movements and demand the same for all children.

The primary question here, however, is can we recreate what has been lost? Is it possible to establish a *new* traditional and tribal culture where children are valued and not lumped into the amorphous category called *teenager*? Can we put the Elders back in the position of respect as guides and teachers of the next generation? Can we fashion a culture where adults once again feel connected to the land, to themselves, and to the great mystery and presence that is generically called God or The Great Spirit? Can our modern culture, shattered like a broken mirror, regain or recreate a cultural cradle rich with rituals and traditions that will return us to the natural rhythms of the world? And finally, if such rituals and traditions could be brought back into force, *what would they look like?* What would this modern day initiation and rite of passage look like?

Here We Go Round the Mulberry Bush

Frustrated by all of these very difficult questions, I at last turned to my own adolescent children. I began listening to their struggles and closely watching their movements thinking that, if I am patient, they will show me what they need most.

Over several months, and then years, I stopped giving them the answers and began, instead, telling them more stories about my own rough waters, about the many difficult choices and decisions I'd made in my life. Many nights we talked until late into the night about how a person fashions a life out of the raw materials we are given. Their level of inquiry and interest in philosophical and moral issues impressed me. My daughter was struggling with several friends who were using crack cocaine and ecstasy—into the rave scene. She was worried about them. My son, a pragmatist at heart, wondered why the heck they didn't just knock it off.

I also began taking the advice of the Elders we'd met in Indian country. "Let the young people do the hard stuff," they said. Let them do all the little tasks and decisions buried within each day. Don't do it for them! I started to see that *doing it for them* was a way of cheating them of their initiation period. Young people need to test their wings, to discover the scope and range of their own abilities. When, as a parent, I take over their tasks, development stops and they become dependent children once again.

One spring I sent my son alone on a road trip to Lincoln, Nebraska, to see his sisters. Before heading out he grinned at me and said "Think of it as a rite of passage, Mom." Thomas was sixteen years old. It was clear that he was excited—making the trip alone was a challenge. Whatever came up, he would have to deal with it. I allowed him to make that trip. Later, he spent the summer working with his father on a construction site, and I saw how beneficial it was for him to be in the good company of his father and other men. He matured greatly during that summer and even more in the following two summers. He was becoming a man.

Sadly, in the fall of 2002, his father was killed in a plane crash. It was the most horrible time of our lives, but I was incredibly grateful that Thomas had had those three summers working with his father.

Over several years I realized something good was happening in my subtle attempts to link my children more closely with their own development. That *something* was not happening from my studies, or from knowing the research on human development, or even from attending such rich ceremonies as the Sunrise Ceremony. The something good was happening in my own home, swirling around the many hours spent with my children talking and sorting out our daily lives. Of course, I still wanted the wide-rimmed drum, the abalone shell on my daughter's forehead—but what I was doing was working.

The Initiatory Moment

Finally, during a collection trip to Hupa[3] country in northern California, I met a teacher named David. I asked him what their tribe does for the young people in terms of a rite of passage. David was not overly talkative but eventually explained to me that the rite or ritual was not nearly as important as the *right initiation*. Initiation, he explained, is the intentional teaching of the young by the Elders and parents that must begin at a very early age and continue on until the child is ready to take his or her place in the community. In his culture, David explained, children are valued as holding the future of the tribe itself—but they are also firmly kept in their place by the Elders, grandparents, aunts, and uncles.

Later, as I studied the family constellation work of German psychotherapist, Bert Hellinger,[4] it became clear to me how important *place* is within the flow of generations. Too often our children are out of order, required to care for mom and dad, one moment taking on too much, the next too little. My father used to keep us in our place by saying we were getting, "Too big for our britches."

Talking to David helped me understand that chasing the pretty ritual or formal rite of passage was not the answer. Without initiation, the ritual is empty.

Wearily, I went back to the hundred-plus pages of this book stored on my computer and deleted all but six pages. I shifted my focus away from the difficult question of what a rite of passage ritual would look like in modern culture and began, instead, to contemplate the full meaning of initiation.

Chapter Two
Challenge—The Heart of Initiation

Malidoma Some' (1993)[1], a medicine man of the Dagara tribe in West Africa, was taken from his village at a young age and raised by missionaries. Later, in returning to his own people, Some' discovered that his place in the village was lost to him because he had not been initiated. In spite of his advanced age, and with great determination, he underwent the arduous six-week initiation and rite of passage ritual of his tribe. When he completed it, he felt as if he was home again at last. Some' (1994) said of our culturally disconnected country:

> I don't know yet what the content of American initiation will be, but I do know what it's going to look like. It has to have a moment of separation from the family and the community. It has to happen in nature and be a genuinely challenging ordeal. Whatever the initiates feel before entering this cycle must be deepened to the point of transcendence, giving them the opportunity to feel whole. Finally, and most importantly, there has to be a strong community ready to welcome the survivors of the ordeal. This welcoming must be massive, not like a simple ceremony of giving a diploma, but a recognizable, wholehearted embrace and valuing of the initiate's power to contribute to the community.

In just a few sentences, Some' summarizes what we all need and want, no matter our age. However, it's a real Catch 22. We can't successfully borrow the traditions of other cultures, but many of us can't recall our own traditions either. Are we then doomed to go through eternity performing empty rituals around meaningless Hallmark holidays—or marking our progress in small, ineffective ways while we continue searching for what we long for but cannot find?

There is a hunger in us. We need connection. We need ritual, guidance, mysticism . . . we need initiation. The more alienated and alone we feel, the more we seek a culture that can guide us. Our young, as we will explore further, feel bereft of this support. In the absence of it, they cleverly create their own subculture and design what is missing.

I recall the significant moments in my own life when an important passage was obtained. In seventh grade I bravely auditioned for a school play in order to overcome my severe shyness. With sweating palms and a pounding heart I took that script in hand and recited the lines. I gained a small role in the play and my life shifted on its axis. Later, in my early twenties I spent six months in Europe. I remember one moment in particular: I was standing alone before a train schedule in Switzerland deciding whether to take a train to Rome or Paris or Barcelona. I felt huge and alone and so excited. What a giant moment that was!

There were also times of suffering, of being uneasy and depressed, entangled in the darker underbelly of my youth culture. In the late Sixties, we sat under full moons with kegs of beer and a campfire on a beach. We sat in dark rooms reading Lao Tzu with joints of marijuana burning. As I look back at the settings we chose, the things we did, it is now clear to me that we sought a tribal presence in our lives.

One day, long after I had moved out of that treacherous era, I was substitute teaching in a high school classroom when a young man walked in with his hair in stiff, rigid spikes rising from his scalp like a helmet. I smiled inwardly. He looked both like a magnificent warrior—and a ridiculous boy—but I admired him. Oh, how I wanted to sit beside him and explain why we now-grown kids of the Sixties are so difficult to shock—our generation wrote the book on self-initiation.

On one of our collection trips we visited Atka, an island along the Aleutian chain in Alaska. The island is home to about 100 people of the Unangax[2] (aka Aleut) tribe. Milt and I stayed in a small guest trailer next to the school. The wind was so fierce at times I thought that poor trailer would tumble over. The Unangax people have blended the Russian Orthodox Church with their own native traditions. We noticed many of the people, young and old, wore a small gold stud pierced beneath the lower lip. Ethan, our host, explained that there is a ritual piercing that happens in puberty to signal the beginning of adulthood.

I thought of all the young people piercing and tattooing body parts in our modern culture and saw again the driving urge we have to find a tribal sense of ourselves. Both piercing and tattooing have, for thousands of years, been part of initiation rituals in many tribal cultures across the planet. The Lakotas pierce the skin as part of the Sundance ritual; the Samoan traditional men undergo extensive tattooing over the lower part of the body.

Like so many other things, this trend toward tattooing and piercing seems to be a visible signal from the young people expressing their need to undergo some tribal ritual of belonging, a test or challenge that may even include pain in order to win their place. When that place is given too easily, without effort and challenge, it is not easily taken. At the risk of sounding trite, today's youth are too soft, drowning in a false sense of entitlement resulting from the prize being given—but not earned. Adults often scorn these alternative practices among the young yet offer no viable alternatives.

What is this web of culture we've created? Does it satisfy? Does it feed not only the body but also the soul and spirit? Are you, sitting here reading this book, finding your life to be all that you had hoped it would be? The truth is, many of us are none too sure of this culture we have created or inherited. We scurry to and from jobs and activities that don't challenge and don't change, a dull landscape of days passing by. We make money so that we can buy stuff, and then run ourselves ragged taking care of the stuff. We seem to just go along without seriously questioning this creature of culture that we have created. We long for our own deeper initiation into something big and mysterious. We are, in fact, the uninitiated. Many of us are still in the lonely place.

Is it any wonder that the young look in our direction with doubt and mistrust in their eyes? Sometimes I simply drive around looking at the monolithic houses we've built and wonder what portion of body and soul (not to mention the earth's resources) does it take to simply keep those houses standing?

When was the last time you were assaulted with a challenge so great that you were completely uncertain if you could make the grade? Did you take the challenge— or slither back to safety? How, then, can we uninitiated adults determine what a young person needs to learn? And then how do we teach and initiate them?

Asking these questions caused me to look more deeply into my own life. It wasn't pretty. I had a dozen books on my computer that had not even been submitted because *what if nobody liked them*? I was afraid to make phone calls that could get me work and support my life. I had an obsession about being a nice girl. *Mustn't make anybody angry or upset.* I passively waited for things to come to me instead of deciding what I wanted and working toward it.

Rather than wallow in my uninitiated swamp, I undertook several challenges myself. I began to speak more bravely, made a few people angry, finished my master's degree, sent the books out and about, etc., etc. I haven't died yet from taking risks—and life advances. Perhaps the hardest part of my initiation was to stand beside my young children after their father died and allow them to grieve knowing I couldn't fix it or change it. All I could do was be there to watch them bear the unbearable.

Socrates said, "An unexamined life is not worth living."

Initiation of the young and the final rite of passage, the event that marks the movement from childhood to adulthood, is the stuff of stories and myths found across the globe and in all forms of literature, religion, and culture. Consider Jack confronting the giant at the beanstalk, David slaying Goliath, the three little pigs off to seek their fortunes, or Hansel and Gretel facing the wicked witch who would have them for supper. Consider Odysseus standing on the shore of a massive lake, undergoing one trial after another. Every culture is rich with quests, hero legends, and the mythologies intended to guide our lives.

This mysterious passage is not only through time or space but is an interior journey toward a stronger sense of self, a deepening of our human experience of soul. It is the young boy facing the whale on a gray sea or the giant buffalo on a sea of pale grasses with nothing but a tiny weapon. It is the young girl moving into the mysterious arts of her sex in preparation for the great moment when she will give birth to the next generation. The themes play over and over again across the globe. A child enters a dense, dark forest—and emerges an adult. The movement has an inevitable timelessness to it.

Initiation is not just for teens. Any time we enter a new stage of life or go through a transition, we again enter a period of initiation. We must all undergo these passages. Essentially, we are climbing the ladder of the soul.

Challenge—the Heart of Initiation

As we have explored, challenge and risk-taking are the twin moons of this passage from childhood to adulthood. It is the times when we are suddenly forced to reach deeply into our reserves of memory, knowledge, and experience. With appropriate challenges, the triune brain begins to branch, grow, and explode into the frontal lobes to bring about a higher level of experience. If there is no risk and no challenge—there will be no growth.

However, growth requires incremental challenges, small steps that move ahead but do not overwhelm. When the risk is too great, we freeze. Children, especially, need strong families and a wise culture around them to guide these steps. They need to feel firmly connected first to the family and then to the culture in which they live. This web of connection provides the safety net that later allows them to walk the tightrope high above their heads. As the child grows, the level of challenge and risk can also grow and, in adolescence, there is a leap forward.

Who better to provide the safety, challenges, and the basic necessary skills than an adult or Elder who has gone the route? Throughout human history, the initiation of the young has been the responsibility of the Elders and parents of those young people.

In ancient tribal traditions, initiation and the rite of passage for the male and female children was guided by life itself. Guidance varied according to the role each was expected to play within that culture—and the roles were determined by the needs of the community.

For instance, in a culture depending upon the land for sustenance, the use of tools and weapons, the methods for successful hunting and fishing took precedence. Survival wrote the subtle laws that evolved over many, many generations, and these natural laws were then passed on to the next generation through the initiation process. However, in spite of many cultural variations, the biological laws took precedence.

Boys were taught to provide food and safety, and the girls were prepared by their Elders to have children, although all members of the community gathered food. Often the boys were challenged with harsh and stringent initiation practices. The girls generally underwent a more subtle initiation. It was not because the girls were the "weaker sex" but because the Elders knew that the young women would undergo their own trial by fire in the birthing bed. In childbirth, a woman faces death. The boys, however, needed harsher measures in order to prepare them to protect those women and children. Without this basic division of labor and expectation, there would be no clan or tribe or next generation.

I use the past tense here with some "tense" confusion and want to remind the reader, and myself, that there are still many existing traditional cultures that continue the rituals much as they have for thousands of years. However, there are also many tribal communities struggling to redefine themselves in the modern world after facing almost total cultural loss. They stand with one foot in an ancient tribal way of being, and another in the realities of this modern world. Both past and present tense are appropriate when speaking of tribal cultures.

Recently, a friend and I were talking about the state of your youth. She is Lakota and was incensed by the rate of incarceration and suicide for Indian youth. I pointed out to her the rates are extremely high for all young people. We finally agreed that if you are Indian—and adolescent—you are doubly damned in this culture.

To tribal cultures struggling to hang on to their traditions, the modern world poses a difficult challenge. For instance, the small community on Atka, while still a very closed community, is also globally wired to the modern age. They have Internet access, computers and a link to all the resources of the mainstream culture. The globalization of our modern society is becoming a major factor in how communities define themselves—and also how they can lose a sense of identity and connection. Paradoxically, the growth of the global family also demands that we redefine how we do culture and belonging.

Regardless of our rapidly changing world, it is still the family and the culture which are responsible for the many processes that turn a child into an adult. Unfortunately, we are not doing a very good job.

In this modern world, the roles between men and women have been muted and blurred. The giant Calvin Klein billboards show the girls looking like boys, the boys looking like girls and none of them looking too happy about it. Our roles are confused. This gender confusion is exacerbated by several other factors of the newly emerging world.

For instance, risk and challenge have been neutered in our liability-conscious society. We are afraid to let our young stray out into that dangerous world. We are afraid to let them risk anything for fear of being labeled a bad parent.

Organized and professional sports have replaced the hunting and warrior societies. Our collective memory as farmers or hunter/ gatherers has turned us into obsessive shoppers, constantly roaming the aisles, baskets in hand, to survey the wares provided so abundantly for us.

Sexual initiation, once a beautiful and gentle unfolding of natural procreation, has either become just another sport or a source of worry, fear, and shame.

The goal of all ancient rites of initiation was to bring the child into the community as a *contributing* member of that community. Rather than being initiated into the role of providing assistance to the family and community, young people now hoard their first paychecks from McDonalds and Wendy's, and plot how to spend the 'me' money, thus entering the role of *consumer* rather than *contributor.*

Is it any wonder that our young people are unable to determine the role they must play, unable to feel the value of their own contribution to the family and community in which they live, and unable to move fully into their own open-ended potential? In this new world, our forests have been laid over with concrete, the giants are long gone, the lands have been tamed, and the mysteries banned. We raise the sword of our own skills and find nothing huge and scary upon which to turn the blade of our own courage and character—and so we turn it on each other.

Malidoma Some' (1994) said, "Initiation is the bridge between youth and adulthood. In my village, a person who is not initiated is considered a child, no matter how old that person is. Without initiation we cannot recall our purpose. To not be initiated is to be a nonperson."

Extending Adolescence

It is clear that today's adolescent is having a tough time growing up. In a summary of research on adolescent development, Frank Furstenberg[3] explains that use of the word *adolescence* only emerges in the mid-20th century when the children no longer took their working place within the family and community but went to school instead. Furstenberg (2000) described a central paradox in this cultural shift. He said:

> To a great degree, the problematic features
> of adolescence and the transition to adult-
> hood are structurally created and maintained

by social institutions that isolate youth from adults; ironically, this is done to prepare them for future roles.

In other words, we have created institutions designed to advance our youth but realize too late that, when separated from adults, they become isolated and, in response, will grow their own subculture.

Adolescence, as a stage of life, was created by the shift in our culture toward formal education for all children—and away from the natural movement of the child into the role his or her parent occupies. Educational systems, as has been well documented, were created to prepare children to serve the industrial age. Unfortunately, this isolation and the creation of adolescence as a life stage have not advanced our development—they have delayed it.

Robert Bly, a well known poet and contemporary teacher, suggested in his book, *The Sibling Society*, that the vast majority of our population is frozen in adolescence, forever stuck with making limited choices based on "me and mine." While Bly's assessment may very well be correct, it presents a terribly bleak view of human development at the beginning of the new millennium. However, in societies as in individuals, crisis, breakdown and chaos are often the forerunners of transformation. Perhaps we can take hope in that and wonder what new uprising of human potential is about to unfold. Ventura (1994) said:

> Adolescence is a cruel word. Its cruelty hides behind its vaguely official, diagnostic air. To say someone is 'adolescent,' going through 'adolescence,' or worse, 'being adolescent' is to dismiss their feelings, minimize their troubles and, (if you're their

parent) protect yourself from their uncom-
promising rage.

I will not spend a great deal of time here analyzing
what has caused society to weaken in this way. There are
enough committees, task forces, and other entities spending precious time and resources attempting to analyze the
factors at play. We could spin the bottle and it would
point at government, schools, television, computers,
rising divorce rates—and it would change with each spin.

Playing spin the bottle won't solve the problem. It
won't bring back what has been lost or chase away what
has arrived. We can only begin by looking at what our
society has become—and then take advantage of our
unique, human ability to adapt to our surroundings and
go from there. Biology won't change. Adolescence won't
go away. However, culture is man-made. We determine
what it is and what it will be.

Chapter Three
Pseudo and Remnant Rites of Passage

What happens to our youth when their need for initiation and a rite of passage is not met, and they are left to fend for themselves?

Paradoxically, two opposing forces are at work here—the need to belong and the need to separate. The young teen simultaneously wants the comfort and protection of childhood, and he or she also wants the risk and challenge of adulthood.

Parents, too, are caught in the same push/pull. They want the child to move forward—and they want the child safely home and in bed.

This tension between two equally powerful forces, belonging and separating, plays its music in so many different ways—from the total development of a new tribal subculture (gangs) to the almost innocent (but still deadly) challenges of who can drink the most Southern Comfort. This broad range of responses is our best indicator of the powerful force behind the need for initiation.

Additionally, young people are vulnerable to advertisers, vulnerable to one another and the pressures of their peers, and vulnerable to the turmoil of their own attempts to do soul-building. No one is exempt from this time—not the pretty girl who gets perfect grades, conforming beautifully to what Mom and Dad want—and not the young male with spikes in his hair and an earring through his eyebrow.

What is most amazing is how well they manage alone. Having been mostly denied the company of adults and Elders, as Furstenberg (2000) described, they manage to create a structure that does the job, more or less. In truth, the subculture of adolescence contains all the important structural elements and subsets of the mainstream culture. Unfortunately, self-guided initiation can sometimes have painful and tragic consequences.

The following pages explore the many ways that we, both young and old, have attempted to hang onto some form of rite of passage rituals and to guide our youth into adulthood. I call these the pseudo and remnant rites of passage.

Peer Initiation—The Pseudo Rite of Passage

In this uneasy age we have young people initiating one another and creating rituals of their own design. Risk and challenge are still evident, but the venue has changed. They challenge one another with such tasks as who can drink the most, who dares to drive the fastest, who will lose their virginity first, who dares to do drugs, pick up a gun, or take on another in a violent fist fight? In the absence of responsible and socially-conscious Elder-based initiation and rites of passage, the young people have simply made up their own.

Any initiation undertaken within a group of peers is a *pseudo* or false rite of passage. In peer initiation the young person is both separating from the parent culture and finding a new belonging in his or her peer culture.

The pseudo rite of passage contains most of the same elements (which we will examine more fully in a later chapter) as a traditionally constructed rite of passage. There is a separation from the mainstream community. There is the opportunity to undergo a test or challenge. Although we are talking about a peer group, there is also often a hierarchy of leadership from eldest to youngest (or coolest to not-so-cool). Finally, the peer community supports its new members in achieving new heights, however misguided those may be.

The primary element missing entirely is Elder guidance. In the pseudo rite of passage guidance comes from within the peer group itself, as does the celebration of the status of the new member.

Essentially, well-formed peer groups become a tribe. This new tribe with its peer initiation allows the young person to define personal identity and form community. We find these new tribes taking the shape of gangs, cliques, clubs, and other socially-organized groups.

For instance, an entire culture can grow around the computer hackers and gamers—or around the chess club. These cultural groups can be either loosely organized or very sophisticated and complex. The behaviors that arise from such groups, as we have seen in both large cities and small towns, are dictated by the group and can be either very innocent or they can evolve into bizarre and violent forms. A group may have its own code which includes language, dress, and behavior as well as initiation and ritual practices. The codes and rules of belonging vary greatly within the strata of adolescent life and will form around common characteristics within the membership. The tribe creates the accepted codes.

Unfortunately, young people are often willing to pay a heavy price to belong. The group may challenge the new member to undertake a task or feat in order to gain membership. This can be anything from auditioning for band or cheerleader, to becoming sexually active, to shooting drugs, to killing another child. What, we must ask, are they seeking that they are willing to pay such a heavy fee for their membership?

It's important to note here that there is a universal tendency in all human beings to seek to belong to a group. We are social creatures, after all. This behavior is not pathological in and of itself. From preschool age on into old age, we take membership in many, many groups, often simultaneously. However, it's when we must *com-*

promise our humanness in order to belong that the question of belongingness takes on larger proportions.

Most cliques and peer substructures are fairly harmless. The rules for belonging revolve around wearing the right clothes or hairstyle and speaking the right passwords of that particular group. However, even these benign subcultures often require the youth to give up a significant percentage of his or her own personality and development in order to belong.

Statistics indicate upward trends in gang membership, adolescent crime, drug and alcohol use, and adolescent suicide. This is an indicator that these pseudo rites of passage simply don't work. When young people initiate each other, there is no substance, no deeper morality, and no inward push toward building character or soul. In some instances peer initiation can lead to death, as we have seen in stories of college hazings, street gang activity, etc.

Youth cannot initiate youth. They haven't gained the skills, depth, and experience necessary to do the job. True initiation must come from a higher level of development than that which the initiate has obtained. True initiation must come from the Elders and adults within the culture.

This is no light topic of discussion but one that requires further research and questioning. With even a cursory glance, we can see that this willingness to sacrifice self to pay a price for belonging continues often far into adulthood. When adolescence extends itself into the adult years, we find fertile ground for individuals like Jim Jones who took 900 of his followers into a group suicide, or David Koresh who stood off the FBI in Waco, Texas to sow his destructive seeds. As these two extreme cults indicate, our vulnerability does not end with the biological stage of adolescence.

I remember an intense period of disillusionment in my own early adulthood. I realized that I had done all the right things, yet I was deeply dissatisfied. I'd gotten my college degree, married a nice man, had three babies, and taken my place as a woman in my culture. Why, then, did my soul still ache with intense longings and dreams? This dissatisfaction extended well into my thirties because my initiation was incomplete.

When my first daughter made me a grandmother, I found myself entering yet another life stage and period of initiation. For human beings this ongoing development travels all through life and ends only with death.

Remnant Rituals

Families have attempted to keep old rite of passage rituals in place. We send our children to church school, have them take their ritual places in churches, or see them off to each new level of schooling. Somewhere between ages fourteen and sixteen we tentatively turn over the car keys and, later, we stand aside as they wear a colored robe and receive that longed-for high school or college diploma. If they make it that far, we consider ourselves lucky and successful parents.

Remnant rite of passage rituals include acknowledging the girl's first menstrual period, the first boy/girl party, the first prom, the first job, the boy's (or girl's) first deer—a whole list of *firsts* marked too often with small sighs of relief rather than with celebration. Included in these remnant rituals are also the child's first extended band trip and the stronger religious rituals such as the Confirmation, the Bar or Bah Mitzvah, and others. Many of these rituals are still very much intact, and I honor their place in our lives. However, they generally mark only one small part of the child's passage into adulthood and are thus limited. This important period of development is spiritual, physical, emotion, and psychological.

In the home many of our initiation challenges are weak and sometimes offer mixed messages. Ours is a culture of contradictions; we push the little ones to read

41

and write faster and sooner, and then pull them back from any true challenge. We give and give and give until our kids are fat and lazy—and then berate them for not achieving more.

This picture of current parenting is not a pretty one. We hand out chores and post to-do lists on the refrigerator so the kids will see them (hopefully) as they go for a snack. We enact arbitrary laws and regulations more as a way to control than to instruct. We study the popular books or we turn over the task of initiation to an educational system that has lost touch with what is relevant and only causes boredom and unrest. All in all, we rob them of the fierce experience of hunting and conquering their whale one moment—and push them off a ledge the next.

When our children reach adolescence and this fierce need for initiation arises, we begin to think our job of parents has become that of a police force constantly monitoring the movement of our young people to insure they do no damage to themselves or others.

If we were to re-examine the remnant rituals, we may discover they contain the potential to gain strength and force as true initiation and rite of passage rituals. Because they happen within the family, community, or church, we could make them grow in intensity and strength to match the intensity and strength of adolescence itself.

When my first daughter was about twelve, she wanted to go to on a trip to Hawaii with her aunt. There was plenty of lead time, so I made a deal with her. If she could earn half the plane ticket, I'd give her the other half. It was amazing to watch how resourcefully a twelve-year-old girl could raise money. She babysat, did office chores, and worked for her aunt. Her focus was astounding. When it came time to get on the plane, she was there, ticket in hand. Interestingly, the trip itself was less rewarding for her than the enjoyment she got from taking the challenge necessary to obtain the trip.

As parents, we need to be constantly scanning the current moment for opportunities to appropriately challenge our children. These remnant rituals of getting a driver's license or taking a band trip could be made stronger and more powerful by raising the stakes, by making them reach a little higher for what they want. If you are going to hand out the dollars, or the keys, or the trip to Germany, what are they going to do to earn it? We need to quit being soft as parents and make our children work for what they want. Somehow having the goods has become a replacement for having the guidance.

Replacement Rituals

In addition to these many pseudo and remnant rites of passage, there are a number of honest attempts to reinstate a way of initiating and testing our young people. I found many examples on the Internet and in publications such as organizations that take young people on a challenging trek up the Gunflint Trail in Canada or Outward Bound, Lost Borders, and other wilderness programs that put the young person through a strenuous course to build strength and confidence. Most of these programs engage the natural world in a powerful exchange—as they should.

These organized rites of passage programs often contain many of the right elements: a learning period (initiation), separation from the parents and family, an extreme test or challenge and a welcoming back. Perhaps the one drawback is that they are not sustained over a period of time but are usually handed out in short bursts by teachers and coaches *outside* of the child's own Elder culture.

There are also many modern extreme challenge rituals such as fire walking, bungee jumping, skydiving, river rafting or rock climbing that test at least one area of a young person's endurance and skill. We also see many adults whose initiation is incomplete undertaking such challenges and benefiting greatly from them. It's amusing to see how popular some of these crazy television programs are like *Survivor* and *The Amazing Race*. What we see are additional signs that our adult population is, as yet, uninitiated.

One weakness of these challenge programs, again, is that they don't necessarily strengthen the link between the child and his family, Elders, community, and personal history. As we'll explore more fully in a later chapter, successful separation can only follow a strong bond with these key relationships.

Additionally, these created rituals generally tend to test only one aspect of life and for a limited moment in time. Initiation is not just a physical test or challenge but must unfold concurrently in our physical, emotional, intellectual, and spiritual worlds. In order for initiation and the rite of passage to be truly effective, it must come from the family and community of the young person and touch on all of these important areas.

Organized sports and other activities within schools and the community may also pick up the loose threads of initiation and provide a form of a structured rite of passage. Activities such as band, choir, theater, sports, debate, etc. often have adult leadership along with the intention to build skill, intelligence, and confidence in one or more areas of a young person's life. These groups are most successful when there is one strong adult individual who takes the time, energy, and effort to treat the whole child and his or her needs. These groups provide a peer group and membership—but with adult guidance. They also can provide a program of personal mastery combined with the long-term challenge of winning a competition, making enough money to take a trip to Europe, or moving to a new status within the group as in sports or band. These activities are also recognized in a positive way by the family and community.

However, nearly all of the above replacement rituals generally grow not out of the family but out of *other* people and places. Once again, there may be ways to strengthen these replacement rituals to encompass more of the young person and his family thus providing a stronger movement toward adulthood.

Initiation as an Act of God or Fate

Sometimes nature or fate itself takes over the initiation of our young. The early death of a parent or sibling, a car accident, a serious illness or other acts of fate can significantly impact the developing youth. Such events force the young person to consider all that he or she is and to seek answers to difficult questions. We should be very attentive to the needs of such a youth. They, through no personal choice, must confront the beasts of fear, sadness, or anger. The traumatic event itself becomes the test or challenge which forces their initiation and the movement toward adulthood. In a paper on higher levels of development, Shuppin and Silverman[1] wrote:

> Many of those who do make the transition to a higher form of existence do not consciously choose this path. Rather, they are 'thrown into their destinies' by circumstances which seem beyond their control.

This simple ten-page paper by Shuppin and Silverman was instrumental in my own development. It suggested that a personal crisis is often followed by a powerful burst in spiritual development, a process termed "positive disintegration" by Kasmirez Dabrowski[2] whose work we will explore in a later chapter.

A divorce between two parents, while not an act of God or fate, can also be a time of crisis and trauma in the life of a child. Divorce is like a little death of what is familiar and comfortable and is usually intensified by the strong emotional content that often attends divorce. Parents are estranged, sometimes angry, and each one is certain that he or she is right about the reason for the divorce. Children can be pulled into the struggle through no fault of their own and become players in the couple's game.

Please, if you must divorce your spouse, leave your children out of it. Allow the child to love both parents freely and equally. When we force a child to choose, we split his or her soul with our own personal anger and failure.

Self-Determined Initiation

Occasionally a resourceful young person will identify a weakness in his or her private sphere of life and set about a course of self-determination to alleviate or resolve the issue. This happens more frequently than most adults realize. The youth is operating from an inner resource that he or she may not recognize until later in life—those critical turning points we all have.

Life richly presents opportunities for initiation and advancement at every stage of life. Such life-changing moments can come to us from a single sentence, a dream, a book, or an action we have witnessed. They also come from having enough maturity and development (no matter our age) to recognize an initiatory moment and act.

I also suspect the self-determining young person finds more support and knowledge from adults than he or she may realize at the time.

For example, as I mentioned earlier, when I was in seventh grade I was so shy I couldn't answer questions in class. I was tired of being stuck in this shyness and was determined to get over it. I auditioned for a part in an all-school play, *The Robe*. After barely surviving the audition, I was shocked to find myself cast in the role of a slave girl who, in one scene, was supposed to strut out onto stage alone and do the *dance of the seven veils*. It was impossible. There was no way I could go onto the stage and shed scarves while wiggling my bottom for the audience. The director recognized my dilemma and instead quietly recast me as a silent slave girl feeding grapes to a soldier in Galilee. Having a part in that play completely changed the course of my life—and I had a little help from an astute drama director.

Along any difficult path we take, there are helpers. This is true for our youth and true for all of us. We take the help we need at the time we need it.

Completing Initiation as an Adult

In the many years of writing this book, I've spoken to dozens of adults and asked them how they initiated themselves or what was a rite of passage in their lives. It usually takes only a moment for people to connect with their own initiation stories. An interesting phenomenon happens when they do—they come alive.

Telling a personal rite of passage story reconnects us with the powerful initiatory moment, those moments when we felt both apart from everything that has previously supported us—and wide-awake and open to what is coming. We can recall the smallest details—what the earth smelled like, what time of year it was, who was around us. Initiation stories sometimes take on mythic proportions in our memories.

What was that moment or moments for you? What was that time when you suddenly realized you were no longer a child, no longer dependent upon only the opinion or actions of others for your wellbeing? When was that time when you were caught by circumstances and needed, suddenly, to find your own way out?

Adult initiation stories often revolve around taking a trip and being forced through circumstances to resolve issues of food, sleep, money, and travel (the basics of life) in some challenging or imaginative way. We can casily gather these stories ourselves by looking at our own lives or asking friends and acquaintances for their rite of passage stories.

A common element in initiation stories is that moment of extreme aloneness when, disconnected from all that is familiar, we feel connected to something larger than our own small self. This enlarged sense of the world is the true prize of initiation and one we will explore more thoroughly in this book.

Also common is the initiatory moment that comes from an important encounter with an older adult. At a time of trouble or disconnection, we meet that important coach, teacher, relative, or neighbor who takes an interest and guides us in another direction. When I was in tenth grade, my world history teacher, an eccentric and intelligent man, made it his mission in life to push me out of my complacent way of being and into a different realm. His strong views, when mixed with my watery personality, created something new in me. Without him I might have sunk more deeply into the dark pool of my youth.

Who is that person (or people) who came along at just the right moment and threw something new into the mix of your life? If you think back, it was probably not their gentleness that moved you forward—but their push. He or she didn't let you rest but threw you beyond your present capabilities.

Try to do the same for a young person. Look around and see whose path you have crossed, and then be willing to step in and take an active role.

Initiation via the Mentor

A mentor is an older individual who becomes involved with the initiation of a young person. Although similar to the close encounter in the previous section, this person plays an ongoing role. The mentor may be a family member but is often someone outside of the family.

This initiation story is so common that it's a popular theme of movies and stories throughout our culture. Think of the movies *Good Will Hunting* or *Dead Poet's Society*. Often when we hear of people who have attained a high level in life, whether in sports, business, or other areas, we soon discover the positive influence of a powerful mentor behind them.

The mentor recognizes the sparking life force of a young person and somehow brings that spark into substantial flame. They push, shove, hold, or support depending upon what is needed. Often the mentor recognizes himself or herself in the youth and through some mysterious hidden process, completes his or her own initiation by helping the young one.

We should be alert to mentoring opportunities within the sphere of our own lives. This does not have to come from a federally-funded program or be a formal relationship in order to change a child's life. Often it is simply offering the right stuff at the right time. We should watch for these opportunities.

Initiation Via the Military

Finally, the military can be a burnishing force that brings a shine to the young person. It has long been a practice for parents to encourage the child, particularly male children, to enter the service for this specific reason—to finish them. However, the Vietnam War (and now the Iraq war) have forced many of us in the current generation to rethink this method of finishing our children—sometimes the finishing is permanent.

Dr. Larry LeShan[3] in his book, *The Psychology of War,* reminds us that the original purpose of government in ancient times was to make war. LeShan (1992) wrote:

> Governments are built on an original design whose major function was to make war, not to maintain or make peace. As an

obvious holdover from this past, every
government today has officials in charge
of 'war' or 'defense' at its highest level.
Nowhere, to my knowledge, is there an
official at similar levels in charge of
'peace'.

In this fascinating book, LeShan says that we engage
in war because it satisfies something essentially human in
us that has to do with both being separate *and* belonging
to a larger group or cause. Like the initiation stories mentioned earlier, war brings a sharp focus to all the blurred
edges of life and makes the soldier come alive in a way
that he (or she) may never have been before. In simplest
terms, LeShan says we go to war because "we like it." We
like being fully engaged in the larger movements of the
world. The military, likewise, serves all the functions of a
rite of passage; there is separation, initiation, intense
training, travel, a difficult challenge and the hero's welcome (hopefully) upon return.

A critical question could be asked here. Is it possible
that our government could polish our youth with peace as
well as war? What if young adults were required to serve
their country—but were allowed to choose the track most
appropriate for them—allowed to serve the global family
in some way? The Peace Corps was an attempt at this,
and the model could be strengthened as an alternative
option to serving with guns.

As we've explored, our modern culture still contains
many elements of initiation and a rite of passage. We are
not so very far away from being able to provide what our
youth need so desperately.

All of the pseudo and remnant rituals presented in
this chapter work in odd, interwoven ways to somehow
bring maturity and further development to the young.
Many of us can recognize our own patchwork passages.

These initiatory moments create a coat of many colors that we wear the rest of our lives. We value those significant moments that led us in a new direction or took us to our current place in life. Imagine if such remnant rituals were strengthened and brought into sharper focus with conscious intention. The question is can we boost these remaining rituals in order to assist our young in making the leap to a strong and healthy adulthood?

For help in considering this question, the next chapter explores the most common elements of formal rites of passage rituals used by indigenous cultures across the globe. By keeping these elements in mind we can examine the remnant rituals to see if they could be made stronger and more relevant to today's young people.

Chapter Four
The Five Common Elements
of a Rite of Passage

Bear Butte sits alone on the prairie along the western edge of South Dakota. Something in the wind at Bear Butte simply makes you want to pray. On one of its upper slopes is the now-closed cave where the Cheyenne spiritual leader, Sweet Medicine, is said to have found the four arrows that became the foundation of Cheyenne law and tradition. There are endless stories of sudden storms arising following the sweats and ceremonies on Bear Butte. Pairs of eagles may suddenly land mere feet from visitors and hover above the ground for several seconds before sailing off. Bear Butte is considered a place of power, the cathedral of the Plains Indians. The trees are adorned with the tobacco ties and colored ribbons from those who have come to pray.

It is to this mountain that Rick, a Lakota medicine man, brings the young men and women who are battling against drugs and alcohol. In traditional Lakota culture, "going up on the hill" is called a Vision Quest or *Humblecha* Ceremony[1]. This ritual, as well as the Apache Sunrise Ceremony and many others, are performed to introduce the young person to the other worlds where spirit and vision *replace* parental guidance. The rite of passage may also include instruction on practical skills and values needed to survive in the modern world.

These beautiful ceremonies are culturally specific. We can't snatch what has been practiced for thousands of years and plug them into our own culture as if it would have meaning and purpose for us. Besides, that would be stealing, and our native cultures have lost enough. However, we can study these remaining rituals to see what it is that works to initiate our youth.

The common age for performing a rite of passage ritual is fourteen to sixteen years of age. This, as we know, is a potent developmental period for young people. These rituals were performed for centuries long before psychology and science had any observations to make about human development. The Elders just knew this was the right time. For women, the time was determined by the onset of menstruation. For boys, the age was simply chosen by the Elders. Even in modern society it is at about age fourteen that the young person passes from middle school to high school.

When I first punched rites of passage into a browser on my computer, the Internet sent me 25,000 possible entries. I narrowed the search by entering 'adolescent.' It gave me 555 entries. I spent a great deal of time scanning these entries as well as other sources on traditional rites of passage ceremonies from many cultures. While they vary widely, I noticed that several common elements of initiation and rites of passage ceremonies emerged over and over again. The five most common include:

1. A period of initiation with preparation and instruction by the Elders,

2. A time of purification of the body and mind,

3. A time of separation from family and community,

4. The undergoing of a test or challenge given by the Elders,

5. And finally, the welcoming back of the young

person into the family and community and a recognition of his or her changed status within that community.

In the following pages, we will examine each element separately with the intention of helping parents or adults to create stronger rite of passage rituals by incorporating the elements into existing rituals and initiatory moments. We will also explore what many Elders considered to be the true goal of initiation—a stronger spiritual connection with the natural or supernatural world.

Please note, however, that we must also be respectful in planning any ritual movements for our youth. It is best when the ritual comes out of natural events after a long period of initiation—and not simply imposed on the young person in an unnatural, New Age way.

One summer Milt and I did a simple ceremony with a group of boys camping with their counselors. There were no fires or drums, no feathers or costumes. We simply had each boy make a *ritual crossing* over bare ground from the "sphere of the mother" to "the sphere of the father," a crossing that Bert Hellinger, a German psychotherapist, suggests is the natural movement in adolescence. It was amazing how seriously those boys took that simple ceremony. Many of them had not seen their fathers for a long time—and some not at all—but their desire to make that crossing was powerful.

Don't try to fake an Indian ceremony. Keep any rituals or ceremonies you might design simple and beautiful without too much fuss—and attach them to already existing religious or social rituals if possible. Keep in mind what the intention is—to steer your child toward maturity.

Element #1: Initiation

Initiation, the main topic of this book, is a multi-varied training conducted over the early and middle years of childhood. Initiation includes instruction, tools for problem solving, a stirring of confidence, and a push toward self-identification and independence. We are preparing the child to take his or her place as an adult in our society.

In essence, initiatory moments are what fill the days and nights of our lives. Each day is ripe with opportunities to guide our children toward making choices, taking their strength, and even making mistakes. Sometimes it is difficult to recognize these moments as developmental turning points. We are too quick to do everything for them, make life easy, and take the conflict away so they can be more *comfortable*. When we do this, they cannot grow into adulthood. Initiation takes place from early childhood on. We must not wait for adolescence but raise the bar day after day, week after week so the child can stretch both physical and spiritual/mental muscles.

Initiation takes place within the total sphere of the child, from parents to grandparents, from teachers to religious leaders. We are all responsible for that child.

I want to distinguish this long developmental period from the critical *initiatory moments* mentioned earlier. Our ability to take these larger steps only comes after we have taken many, many small ones.

When I was fresh out of high school, I went to college in Minneapolis, Minnesota. The summer after my first year I wanted to travel, so I arranged a trip to New Mexico to see a cousin through a ride service at the U of M. The trip went fine, but my ride only took me to Albuquerque and I needed to get to Farmington. I hitch-hiked (a stupid thing to do) and managed to get safely to my cousin's house but realized, later, that I'd done a dangerous thing. However, this trip prepared me and gave me the confidence to travel alone and spend six months in Europe two years later.

We are not parenting a child but initiating him. In one sense, the act of "parenting" was done in a few quick moments. Remember, we are also initiating and preparing ourselves to let go of that child. We have to take a lot of deep breaths and deal with our own fears in order to let them take chances.

Major initiatory moments are preceded by smaller initiatory tasks. For example, in many native cultures a special ceremony requires the young person to undergo special preparations such as performing prayers and rituals, collecting certain plants, sewing ceremonial regalia or items, preparation of the site for the ritual, or the completion of intellectual tests.

For those of us who do not belong to such cultures, we can still create specific initiation tasks prior to an important event such as a trip or graduation. Encourage the young person to consider the upcoming event in terms of how it will affect his or her life. What are his expectations, what does he hope to accomplish, how will he accomplish this, what resources does he need, what does he lack? Push him to go deeper than whether he has enough socks or traveler's checks. Allow him to make the preparations, do the paperwork, raise the money, and become ready for the trip.

Element #2: Purification of Body and Mind

Most tribal rite of passage ceremonies include a time of ritual purification and preparation for the ceremony. This may include many different processes from entering the *Inipi* or sweat lodge, to fasting and/or ritual cleansing in baths. The hair and body must be cleansed, special foods prepared, and often it includes adorning the body or wearing ritual garments and jewelry. All of these movements are intended to enlarge the significance of the event as well as to prepare the initiate, inside and out, to receive what the ritual may have to give.

Certain teachings may be offered from the adults and Elders as well as advice on what to expect and how to meet the challenge. Each small step takes the young person closer to his or her entry into the new role prescribed for them. Part of the purification may include music and chanting to clear the mind and body of residue and to create a harmony within.

How does this purification ritual fit into our modern world? Obviously, we all have habits of purchasing new clothes for special events or bathing and adorning our bodies. It is not a stretch to make the moment even more significant for our young person by caring about what is beneath their skin as well as what is on top of it. Ask questions—many, many, questions. How is she feeling about this upcoming event, what changes does she foresee, does she know what she hopes to obtain from this trip/ceremony/ritual?

When my two youngest children were growing up, we were fortunate enough to spend several summers in an Ashram, a beautiful spiritual center in the Catskills Mountains of New York. It was a wonderful experience to see my children prepare for this time. Sure, they wanted to look nice, but they also sensed that we all had a greater goal in traveling so far and taking this time to deepen our life experience.

One night at the ashram, when my son was about eight, we had participated in a feast and celebration with a dancing circle. There were probably three to four thousand people at the ashram at the time and my children had made some friends. During the celebration, Thomas and another little boy went around and around the dancing circle. I was thoroughly enjoying watching them dance when suddenly they both broke away and went running off. I was worried about what kind of mischief two young adolescent boys could create when they were so fired up from the dance, so I caught up with them and asked where they were going. "We're going to the temple to give thanks," they yelled. They looked half-intoxicated from the dance.

Like other spiritual establishments there was a certain protocol about going "to the temple" and I was afraid my son and his friend would raise a ruckus, so again I followed them. These boys were wildly high on life. They didn't know I was watching them.

However, when they came to the door of the temple, they suddenly dropped all their wild energy, quieted their bodies and their minds, touched the floor in a gesture of respect, went into the temple and, in complete hushed silence, bowed deeply before the alter.

I was shocked at how quickly they had contained that wild energy. I stood outside watching in awe, touched and weeping for their tender souls and hungry spirits.

We needn't fear introducing ritual and ceremony to our young people. They understand it. At the level of soul or spirit, they understand and desperately desire it.

Element #3: Separation from Society

Another common element in a rite of passage ritual in traditional cultures is a time of separation. The Elders literally or symbolically separate the youth from the protective umbrella of family and familiar territory. This time alone acts as a preparation for moving into a new level of being. It is a time to leave the old structures behind and embrace new structures that will guide the individual into further maturity.

Separation is the beginning of the journey toward adulthood. In America, however, statistics indicate that the kids are staying home longer, living with Mom and Dad, or running out briefly only to return to the fold without winning the grail.

Perhaps one of the reasons our young are having trouble separating is that the moment—the passage—is unmarked and unguided in our society. A first break from family is often haphazard and unintentional; a school trip, a weekend get away, spring break, going off to college, or camping. All of these informal occasions allow the young person to leave home, but are often heavily influenced by peer initiation.

In tribal ceremonies, this critical period of separation is not just a chance to "party hardy." No, the solitude and separation required during this time has an entirely different quality to it. In this contained space and time, the young person is often given tasks to complete or specific thoughts to hold and contemplate. There might be periods of abstaining from taking food or water. All distraction is carefully removed to allow the process to unfold from within. Separation might include long periods of seclusion and isolation that can last as long as 24 weeks (the Okiek people of Kenya)[2] or a brief seclusion of hours or days.

Separating the child from his familiar (and comfortable) world seems to be an important beginning of the rite of passage ceremony or ritual. It is both symbolic and literal. It brings to the surface the fears and doubts buried within us. Can I make it alone? Am I strong enough? What will it take for me to survive? The separation period is both a breaking of old dependencies and the formation of a new state which includes both independence and a greater dependence on higher realms.

In some tribal societies, taking the child from the mother is an integral part of the ceremony for both mother and child. Mother must also separate from the child and deal with the fear, grief, and loss that it brings. She undergoes her own rite of passage as she leaves one stage of life behind and enters another.

For youth, the separation may be isolation in a hut or lodge, time spent on a mountain or, as we have seen in many adult initiation stories, a trip or journey. We find this most essential theme in all literature, poetry, and mythology throughout time. The Three Little Pigs must go off to seek their fortune, the prince must undertake a challenge to prove himself, or the youth must leave the home of his or her parents to go on a quest. This theme is universal across cultures. In order to discover what is next—we must leave the world we know behind.

Although we mark this with ritual in a formal rite of passage, we actually undergo separating moments many times throughout life. This adolescent rite is offered only as an early teaching on how to separate and go on.

As I have grown in my work with individuals and groups, I see so many who suffer from an incomplete separation from the parents. This separation is necessary to continue on the human path. We must leave the parents and grandparents behind us, taking only our learning and our connection to the earlier generations. When we stay too long, we become entangled in the past, unable to move toward the future.

In my last year of college, I decided to study in Europe for six months. When I got on the plane to leave, my mother and father followed me right out to the plane. I was terrified—but putting a brave face on things. In truth, I felt as if I had an orange in my throat. It took everything I had not to rush out of the plane and back into Mom and Dad's arms. How important and how necessary that movement was for me. It allowed me to stretch and grow, to find my own imprint in the world.

Element #4: The Task or Challenge

Most tribal rite of passage ceremonies include the undertaking of some task or challenge that forces the initiate to face fear and doubt of his or her abilities. In ancient tribal societies, this was generally more severe and dramatic for boys as I mentioned in an earlier chapter. Historically, it has been the job of men and boys to protect and shelter the women and small children. In tribal societies the Elders knew that the woman would undergo her own challenge in giving birth to a child.

The inner intricacies of many still-existing tribal rite of passage rituals are often not shared with outsiders. They are closely held secrets that only the Elders know. Milt and I found, as we traveled in Indian country, that native people carefully guard their rituals and ceremonies. Generally, non-tribal members are not even allowed to attend or participate.

However, we don't need to intrude on other cultures in order to design or discover the right test or challenge for our youth. Throughout antiquity we find numerous stories of great tasks and challenges. Of course, many involve confronting dragons and Orcs and such, but our modern world has its own equivalent scary creatures. We must all find and fight that demon we fear most. For some it is talking to a neighbor about his noisy dog, for others it is the job interview, for still others it is going six months without a boyfriend or girlfriend.

The test or challenge is the thing we must go through in order to get to the other side. When we have done this, we are changed forever. Offering a true test or challenge is difficult in our fear-riddled society. We are immersed in news and advertising messages that teach us to fear one another, fear our own inner being, fear the food supply, and fear the very world that contains us.

Recently I was in a Wal-Mart rest room where a young woman had taken her two small children. She had her hands raised like a surgeon who has just scrubbed for an operation and was yelling at them with a panicked voice, "Don't touch anything." Her little ones were fearful—both of her and of the hidden enemies in the bathroom.

Fear has become a controlling factor in how we parent and challenge our children. We're under a wicked spell, controlled by fear. This is, perhaps, the meanest and most horrible dragon we must face—fear.

In the fall of 2002, Milt and I made a trip to northern Austria to interview Bert Hellinger, the grandfather of Family Constellation Work. I was stunned at the easy pace and relaxed atmosphere of the small town of Kufstein where we stayed. The shops closed for lunch, kids roamed the streets at all hours, and there was a general feeling of safety around us. I hadn't realized how fear-driven we've become in America. Muggers, shooters, germs, bankruptcy, the IRS, job loss, smallpox, terrorists—we are bombarded with messages of fear by our media. We're afraid to touch one another, afraid to challenge our children appropriately, afraid for our lives it would seem. The first time I went to New York City, I was so under the spell of television that I expected muggers to be handing out business cards at every subway stop. Instead I saw only friendly people going here and there. Never once did I feel threatened.

Fear is not the answer. One of the goals of the test or challenge embedded into the rites of passage ritual is to overcome fear. Castenada (1968)[3], in his classic journey book, *The Teachings of Don Juan*, is told by his teacher that fear is the first of four enemies that we must overcome in order to become a "person of knowledge." Don Juan tells Carlos that the "four enemies are fear, clarity, power, and old age." When Carlos asks Don Juan how we can overcome fear, the old man answered:

> The answer is very simple. He must not run away. He must defy his fear, and in spite of it he must take the next step in learning, and the next, and the next. He must be fully afraid, and yet he must not stop.

In my own experience, fear is often the stuff of illusion and not based on current reality. Fear comes from what we *imagine* will happen, not what is actually happening. To overcome fear, we must be based in reality.

Early in my training in Neurolinguistic Programming (NLP), I made plans to study out in Santa Cruz for five days with two competent practitioners. My plan was to travel to California, rent a car in San Francisco, and drive south to Santa Cruz. While having a cup of coffee with my neighbor lady, I told her about my trip. She was completely baffled, even horrified, that I would make this huge journey all alone. "Aren't you terrified?" she asked me. I wasn't—but clearly she was.

Parents and adults need to confront the reality of their own fears. Robert Fritz (1989)[4] wrote about how "fear of imagined negative consequences" can rule our lives.

Much of my work with clients these days is more coaching than counseling, and I'm struck by how many people feel that making a real life change in a career or relationship will destroy the world as they know it. Within ten seconds of contemplating the change they imagine themselves homeless, broke, living under a bridge—and all alone. This unreasonable fear, I believe, is caused by our own lack of initiation. Perhaps we *should* occasionally destroy life as we know it.

Challenge yourself. What is that thing you fear? What is the reality of that fear? How will you be able to challenge your children if you are unwilling to challenge yourself? If we take our fears and inspect them closely, they generally disappear, melting into the bath of non-reality.

Element #5: A Public Welcome and Acknowledgement of the Changed Status of the Youth

The final element of the formal tribal rite of passage ceremony is when the youth returns to the community with public acknowledgement of his or her changed status. This, for many tribal communities, is a time of feasting, dancing, and celebration. With this change comes recognition, acknowledgement, and a shift both in position within the community and expectation. The child is now an adult—expected to take his or her place as such.

How our modern youth must long for that! The high school graduation ceremony is perhaps the strongest link we have to this element of the ritual rite of passage. Our children are polished and cleaned, adorned in colorful robes, gathered together before the entire community and honored as they take their hard-earned diploma. There is a moment in the ceremony where the entire class switches the tassel from one side of the cap to the other as a visible signal that this change is now complete. After the public ceremony, there is often feasting and parties in the homes of the graduates where the adult child again is celebrated by family and friends.

There is no intention here to disparage this very important moment in the adolescent's life. They've worked long and hard to obtain that diploma and paid a price for it. However, it is possible to boost this important movement by paying careful attention to the above elements and perhaps add (in the senior year?) a more significant challenge that would test them not only on the level of intellect or academic achievement but on the level of personal integrity, spirit, and soul as well. We could simply call it "The Senior Challenge" and make it as holistic and all encompassing as possible with special status recognition for those who choose to undergo it.

Spiritual Development—The Greater Goal of Initiation

Initiation is about coming of age and taking the full challenge of adult life. Our Elders once recognized that initiation was also a unique opportunity, a moment in time in which the young person could be connected and linked to the larger sources of life itself. Not only do the Elders of the community guide the young, but they also look to the Ancient Ones to assist the process.

In our travels into Indian country, we encountered many traditional people who still talk to their ancestors and the spirits that they sense are easily within reach. Often we could not record a community member without the Elders first praying and gaining permission from the spirits. This reliance on the larger forces, on unseen ancestors and spirits, is something that science and even religion have too often forgotten or abandoned.

Once we were asked to produce a video for a project on South Dakota's Pine Ridge Indian Reservation. The organization cares for children and adolescents who were struggling, but before we were allowed to do anything, the woman in charge asked if we would be willing to make offerings to the spirits and ancestors before beginning. She explained that in her culture the children are sacred and that the spirits must be involved in anything having to do with the children. This was not a simple request on her part—but an integral substructure to their healing plan.

Later, I began doing constellation work with another Lakota group. Again, before we could begin I was required to do an *Inipi* ceremony so we could ask the spirits if this was the right time to do this work—and if I was the right one to do it. The spirits agreed, and I began working with their group. The spirits had some conditions, however. They said that before every session we were to pray and smudge and, following the work, we were to enter the sweat lodge (*Inipi*) to thank the spirits and ancestors for their help.

Whether we call the great mysterious source God or *Wakan Tanka* or Allah does not matter to me. Never has a human word adequately named such mystery. I only know that communication with higher forces, the ancestors and the Creator, are fundamental to many tribal cultures and to all cultures.

A second common element we encountered often in Indian country is the deep and loving care of the earth.

The tribes who still honor the old beliefs recognize that it is the earth that provides for us—not the other way around. The land is the Mother. She wipes our tears, heals our wounds, takes us to the center of life, and then allows us to rest with her until we return to the earth once again. We can take the energy of both our ancestors and the earth as a form of guidance in caring for both our children and ourselves.

For example, Elena Avila (2000), the author of *Woman Who Glows in the Dark*, tells her story as a psychiatric nurse who returned to her tribal roots in Mexico. She became a traditional healer or *Curandera*. *Curanderismo* is an earth-oriented medical practice grown out of the blended indigenous cultures of Mexico at about the time the Spaniards arrived. Avila began to integrate her ancient ways into the modern when caring for her patients. In her book she writes of using the earth to heal the trauma of a woman who had been raped:

> I would bury the woman in the earth, all but her head. Then I would stay with her throughout the experience, protecting her from being hurt, wiping away any insects that might come near her face, and reassuring her if she felt any panic. When a person has been so badly traumatized, being enveloped in the earth for a few hours is purifying and allows us to surrender our heaviness to the earth.

On reading this passage, I felt an intense inner comfort at the thought of giving such pain and sorrow to the earth. It seemed right, somehow.

During one of our trips to a small village in Mexico we were allowed to participate in an ancient Amazonian ceremony that is performed to renew the earth so that we can continue to live on her surface. I can't speak of the intricate meanings of this ceremony but can only share the effect that it had on me.

The ceremony began at midnight under a full moon with three dancers coming out of the dark wearing some kind of fronds that clattered like sticks as they walked. They wore cone-shaped hats and were completely covered in the regalia (they looked like small huts). Humming a low rapid chant that sounded breathy and rhythmic, the three dancers were then joined by a woman. They bowed to the woman and chanted and, at some point in the chant, the woman began to wail. Her wail reached far out into the night and caused my heart to skip a beat. I thought of a woman birthing a child, bringing new life into the world. The wail came from so deep within that the woman coughed and choked and then began wailing again. This went on in rounds for over an hour until I felt suspended in some faraway place, contemplating the very universe coming to life. I walked away from this ceremony truly feeling renewed.

It may seem strange in this age of science and technology to consider returning to the ways of taking our learning from spirits, nature, or from the very earth. Our belief systems and our minds want to minimize the power of these natural and supernatural forces and rely instead only on science or medicine to give us our answers. The suggestion here is to take both—but to recognize again that nature (earth) is the *mother* of all science.

It's as if we are making a full circle from the seventeenth century when scientists broke out of the straitjacket of religious dogma to forge their own way. Now, centuries later, we find ourselves wearing another straitjacket—the dogma of science. There is no suggestion in these words to reject all the wonders of science and return to the land, but only to expand our thinking out to include, once again, the larger forces at work.

The Lakota people have an ancient teaching that once guided and directed all of life's paths. It is, "As above, so below." The teaching is that all that happens on earth has a corresponding response in the larger universe, and vice versa. We are intimately and forever connected to the larger forces that operate outside of our physical or visible awareness. In order for life to go on well, we must align ourselves with these higher forces. We don't exist in isolation from all that is around us. It's up to us to find out in what ways we are connected, or not connected, to the natural world.

Earth, with her natural cycles, patterns, and solutions is a great teacher. Water, wind, fire, earth—leaves blowing, trees growing—all have the ability to touch our soul and make it strong again. We have also witnessed her fury when care is not taken with the natural resources—the air, water, and soil. When we read the work of Galileo, Einstein, David Bohm and other great minds of science, we see that they also have learned their most important lessons at Earth's knee.

A Hopi man we interviewed for the *Oyate* series told us a story. He and his grandfather were out tending a field of corn. He was about ten-years-old at the time, and he went to get a drink of water from a jug. His grandfather stopped him and said, "You're children are thirstier than you are."

The boy said, "But, Grandfather, I don't have any children."

His grandfather pointed to the young corn plants standing in the field and told him, "Those are your children. They do not have the legs to go to a drinking place to get their water. You do. So you, as a parent, must give them water first, and whatever is left out of that water, then you can drink. If there is none, then you can walk to a place where you can drink."

In Hopi Country, that way of being is called the *hardway*. I was very impressed with this teaching. In mainstream society, we make life too easy for our children when we should be teaching them the *hardway*. We should be meeting their extreme energy with our own extreme energy in order to prepare them for all that life will hand them later. To do this the parent must have great strength.

What I've come to understand, as this decade-long book project has unfolded, is that we can find the right way toward initiation and a culturally appropriate rite of passage if we return to our own common roots, that of the land, the spirits, and the ancestors. In our souls, we are all indigenous, tribal people. We don't have to figure it out alone. The true goal and the ultimate prize of a rite of passage is to recognize the larger spiritual forces at work, and to understand that, ultimately, we are not alone.

Chapter Five
The Radiant Human Brain

In my thirty years of working with people, I've had a long love affair with the human brain and how it creates and modulates our experiences. My first burst into this learning was through a technology known as Neuro-Linguistic Programming, a model that traces how we sequence sensory experience in order to create our "map of the world." I spent ten years as a teacher and trainer in this work and learned, as I have again and again, that I tend to teach what I most need to learn.

At another time, I studied the work of a researcher named Dabrowski and his "theory of positive distintegration." This brilliant body of work outlines the way in which conflict forces the brain to expand into higher and higher levels of thinking. This theory outlines multiple levels of development beginning with the chaos of a child, moving to the rules stage, expanding to a *questioning* of the rules and finally to what Maslow would call "self-actualizing behaviors" in which the rules must be personally defined and chosen. At the higher levels we would find such great souls as Ghandi, Muktananda, Mother Theresa, Jesus and others.

What I learned from this study was that while the body goes through chronological *stages* toward adulthood, the mind and spirit also go through various *levels* of development. Most important to our discussion, when we do the right thing with our adolescent children, they will come to the place where all of our rules and lifeways will be called into question. It is even possible that we adults may be stuck in the rules level while our children have gone beyond and are beginning to self-define.

When I was counseling clients, for a long time I could not understand why the people I was working with couldn't form a greater vision for their lives, a longer reach toward some higher way of being. Dabrowski's information allowed me to understand that some will only ask for the rules—and then follow them. All the levels of development are necessary but we can get complacent or stuck in one way of being and cease our own development.

It is best when our young people question the rules and that we guide them into asking even better questions. This is an essential part of their development, including the rebellion, the formation of subcultures, and the sharp inquiry into who they want to be when they grow up.

Dabrowski says that when adults are living in chaos such as alcoholism, illness, a violent relationship or a moment of crises, we need the rules to stabilize. He also said that sometimes the movement from chaos to the rules level of development can be like a conversion experience, such as the alcoholic who finds AA or the person who has a born again religious experience and is suddenly "saved".

What is frightening is the number of people who adhere to a strict, even rigid set of rules and never question them. This is a sign of development that has become frozen. We want sharp minds and spirits questioning all the ways of the world. We want our young people to attain this level of development and not one that mindlessly goes along. We want educational systems that are more concerned with encouraging students to ask the right questions rather than stuff the brain with useless information.

The human brain has been called "the last frontier". There is so much we still do not know. When I was in graduate school, I undertook to learn more about the brain and it only deepened my fascination. For instance, did you know the growth structures of the brain, the dendrites, can branch or prune in as little as four days? Or that the brain continues to grow even as we grow older—but that we must keep it well fed and exercised. The alarming rise in Alzheimer's disease is perhaps a warning signal that we are not engaging our own learning enough.

Perhaps most significant in this discussion of adolescence is that we too often think of puberty as a biological event or a psychological event or an emotional event—but it is also the time when the brain is creating ever more sophisticated networks of neurons and dendrites, attempting to engage more of the frontal lobes.

When I decided to revise this book for the next printing, this chapter perhaps needed the most work. I realized that some of my earlier premises needed tweaking. For instance, conflict is often what drives us to reach further and higher, but when conflict turns to stress and chaos, learning and growth take a dive and revert to more instinctual habits to survive. We freeze, fight, or flee.

Several other events have pushed me into continuing this exploration of the brain and how humans learn and change. I started teaching at Oglala Lakota College on the Pine Ridge Reservation and undertook the challenge of helping students who need to get their skill levels up in order to do college level work. Becoming an instructor has forced me to put theory into practice and some of what I am learning leaves me stunned.

Many of my students have had serious developmental delays brought on by poverty, chaotic family systems, early death of parents and siblings and on and on. When faced with the myriad developmental delays, how does one begin?

Added to this is the heavy pressure our educational system has come under with "no child left behind" and the push for test results.

In the midst of my learning curve, I was introduced to the work of Dr. Rita Smilkstein and her book, *We're Born to Learn*[1]. During her long career as an educator, Dr. Smilkstein has surveyed over 7000 people asking the simple question "how did you learn to be good at something." This is a deceptively simple question, but what she discovered was that we all follow precisely the same steps and that this precise learning process cannot be rushed. The delicate structures of the brain require that each neuron build the twig-like dendrites that will then support further learning. Learning comes from practice over time.

This will probably be the topic of another book someday, but I'd like to share some of my observations while teaching with what Rita calls the Natural Human Learning Process or NHLP.

What I discovered over the years is that learning is a healing process. Human beings *like* to learn; we like to be challenged in an environment that is free of stress, humiliation, and time pressure. Learning makes us happy—endorphins released in the fully engaged brain actually make us high.

Learning literally reduces stress when it is allowed to unfold in a natural way. Learning naturally presents the appropriate levels of conflict that make us grow stronger dendritic structures and connections in the brain.

Human beings are natural born learners. It is what we like to do. However, when the natural learning process is messed with—too much too soon too fast—our ability to learn shuts down.

The brain is the seat of the spirit, the mind, and the body. It is our most precious resource.

During my graduate program, after months of intense study into the intricacies of the brain, I finally decided my brain was like a rare, exotic plant blooming in my head, in constant need of care and feeding and the right amount of stimulation (and sunlight).

It prunes and branches within four days.

Consider then, for a moment, the effects of a poor food/water/air supply, television, video games, computers, stress and overcrowded schools sitting on the time bomb of "no child left behind" and the tendency to diagnose and drug our youth.

Human Development as a Diagnosis

In our current culture, over five million children have been diagnosed as Attention Deficit Disordered (ADD) or Attention Deficit/ Hyperactivity Disorder (ADHD). Recently at Borders bookstore I counted thirteen books dealing with this issue. One drug company manual blithely asserts that, "We can now safely say that ADHD has a neurobiological basis—that is, there is a physical problem in the brain. Therefore, ADHD is not the result of bad parenting, divorce, sibling rivalry, or other family-related environmental factors."

This is a terrifying and informative sentence. It frightens me that conferences and educational materials intended to educate are actually advertising products for the drug companies. This same booklet makes no mention of food, allergies, eating habits, educational systems, or ways to ensure our brain stays "balanced." Of course human development has a neurobiological basis, but according to this statement, we must look for the problem in the brain when the child is excitable or distressed.

We are in a time when children are being diagnosed "disordered" by the millions. How terrible to consider treating the potential movements to the higher levels of brain development as if they were an aberration or illness. In August, 2002 an issue of Time Magazine had an article about bipolar disorder and spoke of diagnosing a two-year old with this disorder and putting him on drugs. This trend must be stopped. Parents have a responsibility to read and study the facts of these potent psychotropic drugs before allowing their children to be placed on them—and not depend upon the research provided by the drug companies themselves.

The fragile, developing brain is still a relatively unknown creature. I anticipate a terrible backlash from this rising trend twenty years from now—but by then it will be too late for many of the children now taking these drugs.

In all fairness, I don't deny the existence of true neurological problems. The brain is still a great mystery. In a recent conversation with a psychologist friend, he reports that in the twenty years of his practice, he has never before seen the level of disturbance that he sees in some of the children that have come to see him in the past two years. "Some of these kids are crazy," he said to me. How does a six-year-old get crazy? There are many factors that need to be studied in open, independent research (not product based). We should be looking at the food and water supply, the actual neurological effects of video games, television, and other imputing sources. All are players in this game of the brain.

We have to take care not to abort the new birth before it has a chance to complete itself. Our young people should question and challenge. And we should question and challenge them back. Diagnosing their distress as a psychological disorder is a fundamental error that we can't afford to make. Our world needs their bright minds and highest functioning brains. We need them sharp, ready, and fully initiated.

Chapter Six
What Shall We Do Here?

The first teacher I had in my study of the Family Constellation Work was a German therapist named Heinz Stark.[1] For one year I followed his work in the United States and even did some organizational work for him. I always loved the way he would first face a client in a constellation group, look at them, and say in that strong German accent, "What shall we do here?" His query was so simple and non-threatening, so open-ended that we would naturally begin to allow for any and all possibilities to unfold as we entered the work.

So, what shall we do here? These are our children. These are the little ones we guarded, watched over, and nurtured as babes. Every heart should break when one of them dies because they could find no reason to go on living. Every heart should break when we pick up a newspaper and see a lousy three-paragraph article about a child who has shot and killed another child. These are not juvenile delinquents, not wasted remnants of a no-good society. These are our sacred children! In Lakota country, there is a saying common in ceremonies: *Mitake Oyasin*. It means *we are all related*. One could say we no longer live in tribes—or one could say the tribe just got larger.

I had a friend who, when she was feeling down or apathetic, would say she had the "why bothers." Our society has had a bad case of the why bothers for too long. We have to solve the right problems and not dump endless resources into trying to solve the secondary problems that arise from not solving the true problem. But when it comes to adolescent behavior and development, we are like the blind men describing the elephant. One will say it's a long, flexible appendage; another will say it's a huge wall with a rough exterior. And while we are all attempting to determine the nature of the beast, we have an ever-growing population of angry, disillusioned young people who thirst for honest guidance.

We have traveled quite a distance in this book, you and me. We've wandered around Indian country, and we've taken a look at what is left of our mainstream rite of passage rituals. So, what shall we do now? Let's start talking and figure it out.

Always, I return the loaded question of what a modern day rite of passage ritual would look like. After the many years of working on this book, I have come to despise that question.

What would a modern day ritual look like if it contained all the above-mentioned elements? In how many ways can we steer this sinking boat of culture toward one of our own design? It's here that we lean our heads toward one another and ask the following questions:

- What is the modern day equivalent of hunting the whale?

- What would make a rite of passage relevant and meaningful to young people?

- What is the right age for a rite of passage in our modern culture?

- Should there be a process that begins earlier as well?

- Is the rite of passage ritual different for girls and boys—or the same?

- Should the final rite of passage ritual be individualized or done as a group?

- What characteristics, values, and challenges do our young people most need in today's world?

- How can we create actions that satisfy the need for initiation and rite of passage, and cause positive ripple effects into the future?

- How can we sweep our current culture of the broken shards of dead ritual—and strengthen the remnant rituals?

Unfortunately, I have no easy answers to these questions and invite you to join me in attempting to redefine our culture. This is no easy task. There is no quick pill to swallow, no page to turn, no buck to pass—not any more. Our children are dying or entering adulthood unprepared to deal with its challenges.

Several years ago I went back to my hometown to work with a group of community members interested in revitalizing the downtown. It was a strange experience, walking those streets the afternoon before I was scheduled to speak. Cass Lake, Minnesota, is a small town on the Leech Lake Reservation. It's a beautiful bit of earth with lakes, rivers, and forests—but the town suffers economically and socially. The school I had attended is gone. The stores I wandered in as a child are burned, boarded, or demolished. Grass grows wild in the places that still mean something to the child in me. It was profoundly sad—and yet somehow liberating at the same time.

When I rose to speak to the community that night, I felt very lighthearted. I looked out across those people who were my friends, teachers, and family and told them, quite frankly, that there is nothing here to rebuild. What we have is a blank canvas. This community is free to become anything it wants to be. We are free—free from whatever it once was, free to be creative, inquisitive and energetic.

I feel the same about our American culture. We keep trying to fix old failing systems and boost weak structures when we could be focusing our energy and vision on what we want it to be *now*—in this time and place.

Cultures are constantly razed—and constantly rebuilding themselves. The sooner we turn from the razing—the sooner we can rebuild. The past one hundred years have so dramatically altered the slate of our communities that we can, essentially, pretend the slate is blank and begin anew. It's time to create a new culture based on this new world. We can begin by asking what do we *want* rather than what is *wrong*?

How creative can we be with educational systems, economic systems, rituals and rites? It will take a lot of work between us. It will take a lot of energy and ideas. We will have to stop simply measuring the problems with endless task forces and committees. Measuring the problem does not *solve* the problem. Instead we should analyze our existing rituals whether they are church, school or family-related and strengthen what is already being done.

As this book has evolved, I've discovered that many great minds are at work on this issue. It will *take* many great minds to begin to shift the culture away from one that dismisses the needs of its young to one that encompasses and enfolds them.

I've chosen to focus my own work on strengthening the core of the family with constellation work, which is described in a later chapter, and my writing and teaching. Others are working at the legislative level in politics, in business, and in schools.

Perhaps critical to this discussion is the way in which we approach education. When I entered a graduate program at St. Mary's University (Minneapolis, MN) program in Human Development, I had the richest educational experience of my life. I was allowed to choose my courses and, essentially, to track the *course* of my own learning.

Learning does not happen in slotted chunks but should flow naturally. In this modern world, the entrepreneurial mind—the mind that can see patterns and connection—is the mind that will take us to a new level.

Initiation, the test or challenge, purification, the ritual moment, and the celebration of a changed status—all are part of the whole treatment of the child. As a culture, we have a giant whale to hunt. We must kill off old systems and create new ones. I welcome hearing about any and all means that communities are currently doing to create this new world.

Changing Our Mental Models of Adolescence

A few years ago I borrowed my stepson's car to run an errand. It was after dark and I only had to go to the store. At the time Murray drove a sporty silver Mazda with heavily-tinted windows. On my way home a patrol car came up behind me with lights flashing. I pulled over and waited until the officer had approached the car before I rolled down the window. I still remember the look on his face when he saw that he'd not stopped a punk kid but a forty-plus grandma. I'd not been speeding or doing anything wrong. The officer stumbled awkwardly through checking my license and registration and then mumbled, "Have a good night, Mrs. Lee." After parenting six young people through the teen years, I knew why he stopped me. He figured I was a young person up to no good.

Peter Senge (1994), a management consultant and author of *The Fifth Discipline*[2], said that in order to build a learning organization—in this case a learning society—we must challenge the underlying assumptions or mental models flowing beneath the decisions we make. Mental models, according to Senge, are the "deeply ingrained assumptions, generalizations, or even pictures or images that influence how we understand the world and how we take action." (p.8) He goes on to explain that most often we are not even aware of the mental models that rule our actions and, until we can see them, we cannot change them.

What are the cultural and social assumptions underlying our treatment of the young? What do we believe? What mental models have we constructed that push the young out of our care?

Several underlying assumptions are increasingly apparent. One is that being an adolescent has nearly become a crime in our society. The juvenile centers and jails are full of young people. The insurance companies penalize young people for getting a speeding ticket by bumping their insurance rates sky high. We look at the young with suspicion and distrust. A second apparent assumption is that adolescence is in danger of becoming a psychological disorder in our society. When a child does not fit within the tight parameters of "normal," we diagnose them as disordered rather than widening the parameters to help us understand them. A third assumption flowing under public attitudes is that young people are clueless. We need to take a moment and challenge each of these assumptions with great vigor.

The Criminalization of Youth

One year at my children's high school, security people were hired to wander the parking lots and to enter any open car to search for drugs or weapons. My son, Tom, said one of his teachers had left his keys in the car and the security guard brought the keys to the teacher during a class. The teacher was outraged that somebody would enter his unlocked car and search his glove box. He claimed it was a "violation of his rights."

Periodically, the school goes into what they call lock down and all the students and teachers are required to stay in their rooms while the school is searched. The students have no idea whether the lock down is a true crises situation or a routine search. Many are terrorized by not knowing what is happening.

We need to guard the rights of our children as we would any other innocent person and protest when they are harassed and invaded as if they are criminals. That officer had no real call to stop me the night I drove the little Mazda. He was just looking for trouble. I'm not naïve about these powerful energies that arise in adolescence, but I do object to making it a crime to be young. I believe that the harassment is worse for adolescent boys than it is for girls, but both are targeted.

What shall we do here? We could take notice in our neighborhoods. We could begin to challenge our own beliefs and assumptions about our young people. Are we automatically suspicious and distrusting of a person simply because he or she is an adolescent? We should resist irrational fears and challenge policies that treat our young as if they are up to no good.

Once when my son was in high school, he came home with a new ID card that he had to scan into a machine at lunch to make sure that he was on campus—and not out there up to no good. We had a good laugh because the picture on his ID was not that of my son. Later, a security guard literally cut the pass off of him *with a knife* and then sent him to suspension for not wearing his ID. Can you believe that?

Adolescence as a "Disorder"

There is a massive advertising campaign going on to put people on very expensive drugs for social disorder, uneasiness, sleeplessness, and on and on. Patients have literally entered the doctor's office having made their own diagnosis and practically written their own prescription based on some cute television commercial. Heinz Stark once said, "All diagnosis is a hypnotic induction." We begin to believe in the diagnosis.

Unfortunately, our health care system demands we have a diagnosis in order to be treated, and so we have millions being diagnosed with one disorder or another. Children are the current targets of many marketing campaigns by the pharmaceutical industry.

A large percentage of the popular media have wholly accepted the idea that depression, ADD, bipolar disorder, and many other disorders are caused by chemical imbalances in the brain. This position is quicksand, unsupported by the data, yet we have all bought the advertiser's message. The human brain, by its chemical nature, is constantly *in varying states of balance or imbalance.* Skip breakfast and you're imbalanced. Get only three hours of sleep and you're imbalanced. Worry about a test and you're imbalanced. In fact, we are seldom, if ever, in perfect balance.

Peter Breggins in his book, *Talking Back to Prozac*, (1999)[3] points out that all of these powerful psychotropic drugs have been tested on the *normal* brains of animals. Essentially, their effect is not to *cure* a chemical imbalance but to *cause* one. He tells a most surprising story of the original FDA chemical trials of Prozac. Breggins says that the population chosen for the FDA clinical trials was cleared of anyone with serious depression or suicidal tendencies. Additionally, no old people and no young people were included in the study. Additionally, the published results did not include the fifty percent of the tested population who dropped out of the trials because of the severe side effects. The theory that depression and other mental disorders are caused by a lack of serotonin in the brain is being seriously challenged by current research, but the public thinking has already drifted in that direction.

We have what amounts to designer disorders being created to establish a viable market for the drugs that are being designed. These drugs introduce powerful and extremely toxic chemical compounds into the fragile developing brains of our youth. It is a dangerous situation because of the vulnerability of child and parent alike. Having the problem identified as a *disorder* does something to relieve the guilt parents feel that they have somehow done something wrong. However, it stops all genuine inquiry into soul-building and development.

What can we do here? Just say no. We can begin to take the signals and cues of the body and brain seriously, reading them for meaning and texture and discovering what language of the soul they speak. An agitated, depressed youth is a billboard. His symptoms don't arise from nowhere; they come from something happening in the life around him. If a teacher bores her students, should we drug the student? Parents, adults, teachers, and the general population have an obligation to educate themselves on the realities of these so-called disorders and discover what is truth and not truth.

Adolescence is not a disorder. It is a natural and potent developmental age that carries the young person to the next place in life. They need guidance, support, resources, and challenges from the Elders around them. They do not need to have those adults place the burden of a troubled society on their young shoulders.

Adolescents are "Clueless"

A third trend that is on the rise is the social assumption that teens are somehow clueless. This damaging image is promoted and pushed on the ridiculous television programs and in the advertising that we have today. Movies with a deeper content like *Good Will Hunting* or *Dead Poet's Society* are rare events.

One night my son and I were having the strangest conversation. He was about ten at the time. He said, "God is everywhere, right, Mom?"

I didn't know what he was thinking about, so I said, "Yes, as far as I know God is everywhere."

Then he said, "Well, if God is everywhere and in all things and people, do you think he ever gets crowded?"

His words entranced me. I thought about the underlying constructs of what he was asking. Not only was he thinking about God, he was thinking about the ultimate comfort—or discomfort—of being God.

Young people are not clueless. True, they are given little opportunity to express or explore these higher realms of thought and philosophical inquiry. Like initiation, they hunger for it. They want to know how the universe is built, where they fit in the larger scheme of things and what, if anything, it all means. Is there Good? Is there Evil? Is there some omniscient operator somewhere running this software of human life?

This deep inquiry is an example of the earthbound mortal self trying to extend itself into larger realms, into the unexplored and massive interior of unused brain cells that are the key to unlocking mystery, fostering understanding, and extending the human capacity to create the kind of world we all want. Somehow we've very cleverly constructed a negative public relations campaign aimed at adolescents in our society. How could this be?

What shall we do here? We should think and speak well of the young. Rupert Sheldrake (1995), a well-known biologist and researcher, pushes us to understand more fully the power of the "expectancy effect" in scientific research. Study after study indicates that what the scientist expects, he is likely to find. The same is true of parents, teachers, and adult community members who deal with youth. This negative public relations campaign encourages adults to expect very little of our young people. Likewise, it encourages youth to expect very little of themselves—or the adults around them. This is a dangerous attitude that, sadly, produces results. If I expect my adolescent to be clueless, I'm likely to get what I expect.

I once joined a task force for a program called "WISE" (Wise Individualized Senior Experience) that creates a way for high school seniors to select, design, and undergo a program of their own making. The program, designed to beat the senior blues, is a mentorship and apprenticeship program that builds a bridge between high school and real life. As I got involved in our local WISE program, it became clear to me that we need more programs like this. We could intensify their efforts by encouraging students to take charge of their educational pursuit and not sit like robots in a classroom. WISE students have built handcrafted canoes, worked with doctors, EMTs, and fireman. They've crafted programs that bridge the uneasy differences between themselves and the adults of their community. Both have gained from this experience.

We can build more bridges of this type. We can give each young person a chance to stand and be counted, to prove that he or she is not clueless and is, in fact, a deep reservoir of ideas, thoughts, and resourceful thinking. The next time someone rolls his eyes as if he knows all about parenting a teen, simply say, "It's the most wonderful part of parenting, to watch my young child become a man or woman before my very eyes. A miracle!"

When I entered the Master's program with St. Mary's University in Minneapolis, I was stunned by the learning experience they offered me. Rather than follow a set outline of *courses*, I was encouraged to chart the *course* of my learning. I was told to "Do no busywork." For two years I followed a program of my own design, trashing what didn't fit for me and adjusting my course accordingly. Because I could enter deeply into topics that were of profound interest to me, learning was easy. My courses were not slotted into categories but integrative, all encompassing, taking small side trips into topics that related to my main subjects.

With the internet and the need we have for integrated learning—the push to get the brain to access those marvelous frontal lobes—I see no reason we can't employ this with students as young as sixteen. If I were asked to redesign the educational system, it would be in this direction. Sadly, programs that allow a student to pursue his or her subjects independently are reserved for the "at risk" student and carry a stigma.

Creating a New Public Relations Campaign for Youth

One day on my counter top I noticed that the large and pretty bowl of tomatoes I'd picked in my garden was swarming with fruit flies and had a bad smell. I gently began pulling the tomatoes out of the bowl and washing them under cold water. They were so beautiful. Sure enough, one large tomato had ripened too quickly and was causing the problem. With this rotten tomato I had to take serious measures (I threw it out), but the rest were still perfect. I also had to recognize that it was my own neglect of the bowl of tomatoes that had caused the problem.

It's so important not to paint all young people with the dark brush and palette of a few unfortunate or troubled teens. This public relations campaign against youth must be contained and controlled by any or all means possible. We act as Dr. Frankenstein must have reacted when his creature first sat up on the laboratory table; "Oh my God, what is this I have created?"

Much of the problem-solving our society engages in has to do with trying to squash symptoms rather than resolve fundamental cultural issues. Rising rates of teen suicide, gang membership, violent crimes perpetrated by young people, teen pregnancy, overflowing prison and juvenile centers all point a hefty finger at the need for a lasting cultural change. We can't afford to wait. Every year the already staggering amount of resources required by our society to deal with these overwhelming problems increases.

What shall we do here? A few suggestions:

- Allow a natural, strong image of the young person and his or her role in society to emerge and grow stronger

- Listen more and stop blaming the young for what they did not cause and cannot change alone

- Recognize our loss of power as parents, and stand again in our place behind and not against the youth

- Offer respect and honor for their stage of life and not poke fun or ridicule them

- No longer allow televisions and movies and magazines to create the common image of the "teen werewolf"

- Give them their right place within our society

- Challenge our social assumptions and redefine the normally developing energy of the adolescent as magnificent

- Redesign our educational systems to encourage brain development and not stunt it

Adolescence is poetically layered with the language of the soul. The questions, *Who am I? Where do I belong? and What is the cost of my belonging?* are fundamental. Sometimes these feelings disguise themselves as depression, sadness, despair, anger, and grandiosity. This is the stuff of soul-building, the direction finder that leads the way toward greater integration and wholeness. The call of the higher realms of thought and being are the carrot in front of our cart. It's important we not judge the disguised appearance of the soul's deepest movements.

While researching the themes of this book, I stumbled across another book by Pearce called *Evolution's End*, (1992)[4]. Pearce is a thorough researcher and has been a favorite writer of mine over the past two decades. In the progression of his books, he has perhaps looked more deeply and holistically at human brain development than most other individuals. After writing *The Magical Child* (1986), he came back with expanded understanding of what he calls post-biological development—or development beyond biology—and wrote *The Magical Child Matures. Evolution's End* extends his understanding even further. Pearce is always interested in what nature had in mind for us. What is her blueprint? What has been coded into us regarding our own human development?

In the book on evolution, Pearce suggested that the brain is not just a processor but a receiver linked into larger bodies of information which he lightly calls "soup sources" that exist beyond the body. With proper growth and development and an adequate push from the environment, the brain can actually extend its neural receptors to receive information from these larger sources of information outside the body. This was the goal of tribal Elders when they took the boy to the mountain and left him there for three days without food or water. They wanted not a compliant, good boy but a young man connected with the ancestors and the realms of spirit and soul.

Initiation and the rite of passage are not only about contributing to the community; they are also about finding the powerful links between this, the mundane world, and the larger realms of spirit, soul, and the greater forces of creation itself. This moment of human development cannot be forced. It can only be prepared for, like tilling the soil in preparation of the later harvest. The opening of adolescence is the beginning of this moment.

Examining Your Own Mental Models

I never did build a rite of passage ritual for my daughters. As I've explained here, we took off on the trail of our ancestral line through the constellation work, storytelling and initiation. However, I did slowly become alert to what I call "initiatory moments" in my adolescent children. In fact, as I think about it, it is exactly what I do for my clients and workshop participants. I watch for a soul on the move toward some new level and try to support that movement whenever possible.

As parents, our job is to make them face the difficult questions head on. We can push them out when things get a little too soft. We can close the pocketbook quietly and ask them, "What is your plan for getting that car/trip/stereo that you want?" We can tip the scale of give and take back in our own direction—give less, ask (or demand) more of them. Additionally, we can get more involved in our communities and neighborhoods and speak up when the negative public relations campaign against youth gets too noisy.

I've asked many adults what they think about youth and they say such conflicting things as, "Age envies youth" and "Age idolizes youth." It seems ironic: if we envy or idolize youth, why do we treat them so badly? Perhaps the truth of this is that we adults are clueless and uninitiated.

What are those dreams and visions that you had as a young person that are as yet unfulfilled? What is your greatest fear, and what could you do to test and challenge that fear? What is it that you long to be doing but are not? What stops you? When I ask this of a group, I don't allow them to use time or money as convenient excuses about why they can't seem to bring about the kind of life they most want.

One of my spiritual teachers says that the only thing we can give to another is our own state. We cannot give what we have not obtained. We need to hunt our own whale. As adults, we need to look inward towards our own soul-building and our own development to find the gaps and fill them in like chinking in a log cabin. We need to discover our own sense of self, our own courage and responsibility. How can we teach accountability when lurking in our purses and pockets are credit cards maxed to their limits? How can we teach restraint and self-discipline when we overeat, over drink, and overuse the resources of this planet? How can we teach compassion and understanding when we so quickly dismiss our own young people? We must complete our own initiation.

In the current state of our culture, it's as if the young people are to blame. Senge says that a common archetype of organizations is to "shift the blame" to another part of the organization. Have we taken the problem of our own lack of initiation and laid it on the shoulders of our youth? To challenge the assumptions that are breaking down the foundation of our culture and society, we need to look into the mirror to discover what fears and unrealized longings are sunk deep into our own hearts. We need to strip down to a loincloth and a bare stretch of ground and have our own vision quest.

It has been my experience with clients, both young and old, that a step back is easier to make than any step forward. Forward movement takes a tremendous gathering of resources and great courage. When confronted with the possibility of bringing forth our brighter, higher nature, we are faced with a fear that is so universal as to send us running for the shadows again.

Initiation is not an event but an ongoing alchemical process. Each fear, doubt, and pocket of self-hatred must be brought to the surface and burned. We need to be purified and tempered in the fire of experience if we are to gain any strength of soul or self.

Do a personal inventory and be painfully honest with yourself. Ask yourself the following questions:

- Am I able to build and sustain intimate relationships with my partner or other people?

- Am I giving any of my vital energy to old angers, resentments, and relationships that have ended?

- Do I have work that satisfies all parts of me and supports me in the world?

- Do I have patterns that take me to the edge of something brand new only to pull me back again, and keep me in the old way of being?

- Do I have a future vision that extends beyond this week, or this month? What is it?

- Am I able to take the strength of my ancestral line on both my mother and father's side? Do I respect and honor their fate without childish resentment?

- Am I a victim of circumstances—or do I have a sense of strength, power, and choice in my life?

- What do I have to contribute to my culture, and am I doing it?

- Am I able to do my life without addictive support from substances, gambling, shopping, etc.?

If your inventory reveals the uninitiated youth in you, consider that buried within your own soul is an unfinished child or adolescent seeking a way out. We find our way to those lost aspects of our Self by examining our darkest thoughts, our fears, sadness and grief, and the greatest yearning of our own heart. We don't wander into our stored memories to uproot or remove them or to find whom to blame, but only to complete what may have been left incomplete so that we can re-engage our own initiation. We approach our past with respect and curiosity to discover what those hiding younger parts might want from us. We, essentially, initiate them.

Another revealing technique for self-discovery is to scan the qualities and characteristics in others that irritate and infuriate us. For instance, if your boss is stubborn and must always have her own way, perhaps you are stubborn and insistent on having your own way. If your four-year-old leaves his junk all over and it makes you crazy, see where your own junk is. This simple mirror technique asks, "How am I just like that person who irritates me so much?" It can sometimes be painful when we uncover our own flaws and weaknesses, but it is worth the effort.

Finally, don't forget to discover and strengthen the parts of you that are vitally alive and burning like warm flames within you. Look to your own creativity, the simple desires, or the love of beauty, nature, or music that sleeps within. When my daughter had her senior picture taken we pulled my old senior portrait out and were both stunned to discover how we resembled one another. It was most shocking to me because I think of my daughter as pretty and very loveable. This was not a feeling I ever had about myself at that age. I'm not sure why, but I was never *enough* to myself: not thin enough, smart enough, ambitious enough. It's a lesson I'm still learning as I continue my own initiation.

When I was in my early twenties I decided to attend a writer's retreat to see what it felt like to be in the company of writers. I was a closet writer and had been for many years, but I was afraid to test my tender talent before the eyes of *real* writers. For three days I went to the phone to register for the retreat. I'd lift the receiver only to drop it again in its cradle. It was awful. I was terrified that I'd somehow find the tiny flame of my desire doused by criticism. I spoke harshly to myself saying things like, "Who do I think I am, anyway? What kind of a fool . . ."

The self-torture was terrible. Finally, like the seventh grade me who finally tried out for the play, I made the call and even entered a short story to be critiqued by the experienced writers in the group. I attended the retreat and was stunned (and elated) when the older woman who critiqued my manuscript called me an accomplished writer. And, almost miraculously, for the first time, I believed that about myself.

Initiatory moments require something of us. In all we have explored, the rite of passage must have a test or challenge if we are to win the prize of the initiation. We have to do that thing which scares us, which we think we are incapable of doing, which some nasty voice in our head tells us that we are crazy to even attempt. Go ahead and start that business, take that trip alone, go back to school, or take up that paintbrush. Just do it.

When we have done this, then we may, at last, have something of value to offer our young ones. The care of the young soul, whether it be our own or that of our child, includes supporting them through the anguished periods of darkness without judging harshly—and without automatically thinking that we must be doing something wrong as parents. This is a selfish stance concerned only with our own measurement as parents. If our children are in a dark moment of the soul, it may mean we have done it exactly right. In our deepest fears and longings are our greatest gifts. If we never turn in their direction, the gifts remain undeveloped and languishing. This can only lead to real despair and depression.

When we have attended to our own inner initiation, we could also consider what, in this modern society, is the whale we must hunt? From studying many of the futuristic books that predict the trends of the 21st century, we can see that our children need to be able to think freely with those little-used frontal lobes of the brain. Our children need to see beyond their own small world and to think holistically and systemically in order to better judge the effects of a decision in the moment. They need to be flexible, able to cope with changing economies, changing careers, and a constantly shifting global society. These are the whales that our children (and yes, we ourselves) must hunt.

When the twin towers of the World Trade Center collapsed during the terrorist attack, my son pointed out to me that the date of the attack was 9-11, the same number that we use to call in an emergency. Tom was already looking for patterns that connect and speculating about what the larger meaning of this date held for our society. He was beginning to hunt his own whale.

Chapter Seven
Strengthening our Cultural Fabric with Ritual and Stories

When my son was just tiny, we formed one of those little rituals that, after awhile, you can no longer even recall its origins. At bedtime I'd pull the blankets up around his ears and then, rather than saying good night I would say *manana*, the Spanish word for "tomorrow." It is such a simple little word but so forward looking, sending the energy of this day into the next. Sometimes, I'd walk down the stairs already anticipating what good things tomorrow might hold.

Now my "little" son stands a full six inches above my head and is striding toward manhood with a speed that makes me dizzy. I've a huge regard for this nearly 18-year-old man-child. Every day I see him ask questions, inquire deeply, and grapple with reconciling the restless movements of his body and soul with a school desk too small for him.

Oddly, his late evening routine of chores, homework, and shower still often ends with him tromping up the stairs, turning his wet head, and saying *manana*. I'm convinced that this tiny, positive ritual acts somehow like a silver rope across the rugged, mountainous terrain he now treads. It ties him to who he is and all that went before, even as he moves forward into what has not yet been mapped.

Recently I heard a wonderful Elder Lakota woman speak at a workshop. She is mother, grandmother, and great-grandmother many times over. In her talk about parenting she said we should always use words like "sweetheart, precious, honey, pretty one" when we speak to our little children. When we use these words, she said, we call their young wandering spirits back to us. According to her the spirit of a young child is always wandering off, exploring other realms and tracking elusive thoughts and ideas. It's important that they be able to find their way home again. When we yell or use harsh words, the child can't find his or her way back to us.

This is what the small ritual with my son has done. When I say *manana* his spirit is called home again from wherever it has strayed. He remembers both where he has been and where he belongs.

Family rituals and storytelling cost nothing but a little time and intention. Once formed, all members of the family happily anticipate them. My father used to come into my room each morning when I was a small girl and say, "Good Morning, Glory." I cherish this memory, so filled with his familiar smile and gentle voice, calling me back out of my dream world and into the new day.

Small rituals create a strong web within the family that ties each member to the center. It's just as easy to establish daily routines that include these ritualistic moments as it is to create the opposite—harsh bellowing to one another and painful patterns that disconnect rather than connect. Be conscious. Watch for small *good feeling* patterns that could easily become the family's rituals.

In the previous pages we've sorted numerous ideas for how to recognize initiatory moments and develop-mental levels. Now we return to the inevitable question of culture itself. How can we strengthen the fabric of our culture, whether within the family or the larger community, so that initiation rituals emerge naturally?

Using Ritual to Strengthen Culture

We can find many fabricated rituals within the marketplace of New Age workshops and ceremonies. We can, in essence, *buy* ourselves a rite of passage. This is an odd artifact of our modern culture. I can buy a sweat lodge ceremony, a healing ritual, a trek into the wilderness, a vision quest . . . but when I turn to the natural movements within my own culture, I find little to support me.

Maria T. Stadtmeuller, in an issue of the *Utne Reader* (Nov. 2001), wrote of her search for an authentic way to worship nature.

> Like a lot of people seeking some spiritual connection to the natural world, I read up on Native American spirituality, but it felt like a cultural trespassing to demand a seat for my white ass in the sweat lodge. What I am, I realized, is spiritually hungry and European.

Her article made me laugh. I've also attended crone birthdays and solstice celebrations, and had the same embarrassed feeling of wanting to sneak out a back door. My sense is that rituals that have not emerged naturally from the cultural fabric appear in our midst like a cartoon. They feel imposed or arranged instead of deep and meaningful. Perhaps what is most hopeful about the abundance of these imposed rituals is the charged signal from our society that we need, demand, and want a more sacred and meaningful way of being.

A young client told me about her own rite of passage ceremony. When she first noticed curly hairs growing in a certain region of the body, she shyly asked her mother about it and her mother decided that her daughter needed a rite of passage ceremony. Mother took daughter to another woman friend and together they devised what they considered an appropriate celebration to mark the daughter's new status. Without the support of centuries of cultural preparation, the daughter found the ritual to be humiliating and embarrassing.

Rituals don't have to be elaborate or ancient to be meaningful. In fact, many of us have formed small rituals around daily living that call our souls to the sacred, natural world. We light a candle when we take a bath or sit down to meditate. We pick that first tomato in the garden, and hold it up to the sun with a smile. We ritualize school shopping each fall to give the child a special entry into the new school year. All around us are the small rituals that have emerged naturally from the culture that contains us. We can, however, create rituals with more conscious intention.

Research indicates that children raised by families (even dysfunctional families) that maintain a sense of ritualized family routines develop into stronger adults. A regular seat at supper, meals at a certain time, going to church, a Saturday morning special breakfast . . . all of these are rituals that strengthen families. Families that grow their own rituals are stronger than families without ritual. This small "blip" on the social screen is so simple as to be almost unseen by most of our culture.

Ritual moments can grow naturally from the movements of daily life without being imposed in a false way, like saying *manana* to my son each night. We can let the rituals grow naturally around us and mark them with special words, actions and movements. In *Calling the Circle*, Christina Baldwin (1994) wrote,

> We all have rituals in our lives; we have simply forgotten that in our original way of living on the earth, these rituals were sacred, not secular. These rituals were designed to remind us over and over again of our true relationship to life: that of a grateful, amazed supplicant at the feet of mystery. (p. 11)

The Ritual of Telling Stories

During our travels into Indian country, the native people constantly reminded us that originally theirs was an oral culture. The passing on of traditions and cultural ways was accomplished by telling stories. Dark winter nights, especially, were reserved for these special times but the telling of stories was done at any time. In other words, one key to successful initiation is storytelling. This ancient art, practiced since man first conquered language, can introduce the young spirit into the mysteries of his or her world. Through storytelling, we can begin to reinstate the process of initiation of the young in American families.

In the early days of determining how we wanted to present the material we were collecting for the *Oyate* series, we thought of all the possibilities. We could try to stuff it full of complex tribal history, of musicology, anthropology, theory and thought. We could strangle it with our own narrative style. We could pose and postulate and huff and puff.

In the end, we decided that there was nothing more powerful than the stories the people themselves had to tell us. Hidden within the stories are the deepest philosophies, the most intricate historical details, the most complex intellectual processes, and the truth of evolution and human development. It's all contained in the stories.

Since the beginning of time elders, teachers, saints, sages, and parents have used stories to transmit information. Through stories, we teach. Through stories, we learn. Stories are the distillation of human experience, where all the excess is cut away and only the gems are kept.

This realization, of the power of stories, caused me to again shift my eyes away from the pretty rituals, the abalone shell on my daughter's forehead as the only significant ritual. In the end, I understood that the ritual of telling my own stories was and is initiation. And so I tell her the story of the time I had to wage my own battle with shyness and feeling inferior, the time I auditioned for the part of a slave girl in an all-school production of "The Robe"

. . . I was in seventh grade. I couldn't answer questions without stuttering and blushing and wanting to run. I couldn't make new friends. Couldn't talk to boys. Couldn't answer a question in class. I didn't know how to change who I was—only that I needed to change. A notice appeared on the wall announcing auditions for the all school performance of "The Robe." It took everything I had to show up in that classroom, pick up a script, stand when the director said to stand—and read the part. To this day I am not sure how I actually accomplished it, only that my desire to crawl out of my shy shell was so powerful that I couldn't not do it.

The plot of the story? Girl meets her demon (shyness) head on and wins. It's one of my stories. I still remember the knot of nerves, the urge to pee, and the sweaty palms of that audition. I can also remember the many weeks of rehearsals, finding new friends, and beginning to flower in a different environment that was the prize of having defeated the demon.

We all have rich reservoirs of stories like this where we discover a character flaw or weakness, devise a plan to overcome it, and then implement that plan. Truthfully, these stories make up the complex web of strand, and string, and gauze that eventually make us an adult. We should tell these stories to our children. We can tell them of times we were scared, angry, intimidated, shy, hurt, stupid, cowardly, or depressed. We can tell them of our humanity. And within the story we can tell them *the way out.* From our stories they can add the texture and fabric of their own experiences. And they can learn from the stories.

Because we modern adults are ourselves too often uninitiated we somehow feel unfinished and insecure. We feel we must stand on a false cliff of authority and spout off the rules and laws of human being and ask our young people to swallow them without chewing. When we tell the *stories* behind the natural laws and evolution of our own existence, we begin to build context and depth; we trace the path of experience that caused a rule or a natural order to become such. We share with our young person the process by which we gained maturity.

At the heart of any culture is the story. It was the story that Jesus Christ chose as a means of teaching his disciples. They call them parables. It was the story that Socrates and Plato used to encase the teachings of their great philosophies. It was the story that gave Bill W. from Akron, Ohio the means to help other alcoholics in the program that later became known as Alcoholics Anonymous. Bill W. discovered that if he *told his story*, what it was like, how it is now, to other alcoholics, some would almost miraculously start to recover from the drinking habits that were killing them. It is the story that sustains book publishers, magazines, Hollywood, television and most forms of written publication. It is the stories that have brought our radio series, *Oyate Ta Olowan*, a fair measure of success in the marketplace of public radio.

Stories are one of the simplest, most sublime ways that human beings have of connecting with one another. Through stories we build intimacy, transmit information, pass history from one generation to another, and use humor, example, and characters to teach. Stories have the magical capability of presenting new paradigms, setting examples, highlighting important philosophical ideas, and teaching ways of being. With a story, we can illustrate how a character made foolish mistakes—and lived to tell about them. We can detail the process by which a character arrived at a certain conclusion.

Stories engage all the senses, travel through time, and allow the brain to form intricate and subtle connections deep within its buried lobes. Sometimes they simply sum up our experiences. It makes sense that in my long search to create a current and active process for initiating youth into adulthood, that I would eventually end up at the story.

During this long decade of researching this book, my husband and then 12-year-old son, Tom, had a bet with one another to not watch television for a year. The television went off in our house pretty much full time since my daughter and I weren't big fans of the tube. We moved the television into Lisa's room and left it there.

Throughout that year many things began to happen. My husband picked up more novels and magazines; evenings consisted of many hours of quiet time that hadn't previously been there, and we all talked more. Tom and Lisa traveled with us on some of our collection trips and we spent many hours in cars and planes. I didn't realize it at the time, but we began to tell many more stories. As I think back, most children I've known love a story. To get the attention of any child all you have to do is start a sentence with, "What I remember most about the day you were born is . . ." In fact, perhaps the most powerful words in any language are, "Once upon a time . . ."

For us, the stories eventually led into other forms of discussion. Why do people act in certain ways? Why does the natural world operate the way it does? Why do people go to therapists instead of just making up their minds to be different? Once we spent two weeks at an ashram in New York State and the four of us, (Milt, Tom, Lisa, and I) sat in our room and told the stories of the saints and sages of India long into the night. Still, in spite of the increase of conversation in my family, I wasn't really paying attention to this process. I was like the Queen who searches the kingdom for her missing diamond necklace only to discover she had been wearing it beneath her robe all along. Part of the answer was before me throughout the long search for the *right* initiation and rite of passage ritual.

Then, in April of 1999, my mother unexpectedly became very ill and was taken to a hospital in Fargo, ND. By the time my family and I arrived from Rapid City, SD, she was dead. I was shocked and hurt and grieving deeply. My sisters and I went through my mother's house bagging clothes and setting small items aside for grandchildren and children to choose mementos from. We found that what we sought most were *stories* that somehow related to us.

In her purse was a Christmas card my daughter and I'd made the previous Christmas with a jolly picture of mom's first great grandchild on it (my grandson). One edge of the card was frayed and torn—evidence that she had carried it in her purse during the months since Christmas. A story! Our greatest find was a small spiral-bound recipe book in which my mom had taken the time to write one card for each of us that had small details about the day we were born. There were eight small cards—one for each of us. We were ecstatic with our gift.

Again, without exactly naming it, I realize now that we were starved for her stories; family stories, Mom stories, stories about ourselves, stories about her life, our father, her mother—ANY stories. In the days that my brothers and sisters and I spent together directly after our mother's death, we also told stories. Everyone that came to the funeral told stories. It was part of the grief process.

Three weeks later my daughter had a second child. The first thing I wanted to do was call my mother and tell the story of the birth of her new great grandchild.

Birth. And death. Everything in between is a story.

It was then that I realized I'd been looking at the wrong parts of native culture for the answer to my question about adolescent initiation and rites of passage. I was looking at the Sunrise Ceremonics, the Vision Quest, and the Sundance when what was really at the very pulse of both of these ceremonies are the *stories that are passed on from one generation to another.*

I speculated that perhaps the lack of relevant stories is what has driven the stake into the hearts of our own poor culture. We don't talk or tell stories to one another anymore—not with any intention or purpose. In fact, we let others do our storytelling for us. The surge of technology in this modern age has shifted our hunger for personal stories to screens; movie screens, television screens, computer screens, ATM screens.

One of the greatest traditions and legacies from all ancient cultures was the passing down of oral traditions through stories from the old to the young. That is what we are missing. When we interviewed Bert Hellinger in Germany, he said Americans are restless because they seek their ancestors and family stories.

One night, to test the theory, I sat on the burgundy couch in my living room with my two young teens and began a story with "I remember when . . ." Two hours later I practically had to peel them off the couch, and push them into their bedrooms to get some sleep. They wanted more. They will want more. The question is how can we tell better stories?

What if we had a better approach to storytelling as a means of initiating our young people? This may sound very simplistic, and it is my hope that the simplicity of the plan not detract from its merit. It's the sheer simplicity that makes it so beautiful. It costs nothing, requires no special training, and is at our fingertips. Can we learn to initiate our young people by telling stories?

Essentially, a story mirrors the human thought process. It has a beginning, a middle, and an end. It has conflict that must be resolved by using a variety of available resources. The character in the story must develop the discernment and understanding of how best to use the available resources by sorting, experimenting, choosing, tossing, or using.

When we think about our young people—or ourselves—many tend to think in terms of *what* we want them to be rather than *how* we want them to be. In truth, the *what* comes out of the many years of *how?* Behind every successful human being, whether they are an entrepreneur, doctor, lawyer, writer, manager, or parent (the what), is a complex grid of strategies (the how). In every moment of every day we employ strategies to try to solve or resolve the many situations and conflicts that arise with each task we try to accomplish.

Initiation then is the ability to impart to our young people (or ourselves) strategies that allow them to glide smoothly through the confusing market place of today's world. These young people will have to navigate the uncertain waters in a sea of choices about careers, relationships, money, politics, right food, and keeping the environment alive. And they will have to do so while their senses are being battered with a thousand conflicting messages per day (or per hour). Research constantly indicates a growing population of disoriented, depressed, stressed out, and alienated citizens of adulthood.

Traditional, ancient cultures had tough choices too, but their own natural environments limited these choices. Our modern youth must not only hunt the whale—but save it as well.

It's amazing to me how we can continue to think that sheer authority—correction and harsher punishment—will somehow give our young people useful strategies for life. It doesn't work. The quickest way to shut down a young person's mental and spiritual development is to tell them what they *have* to do or be. Even better yet, scream it at them. It's the classic case of "Do what I say—not what I do." A great deal of empty space has been created between our young people and the teachers, parents, and the authority figures in their lives.

This gap makes learning difficult if not impossible. Children learn by modeling. They will model our every behavior, action, and ways of being.

Let's begin by using storytelling to simply close the distance between us. In the wealth of materials for helping writers become storytellers, one of the main suggestions to us is to show, don't tell. The story illustrates with words what you want the listener or reader to hear, taste, smell, see, and touch. It's both evocative and suggestive. The story allows us to communicate in a way that creates a link between us and the child, between the child and his community, and most importantly, the child with his or her own character and identity.

In addition to the desire to build useful and effective strategies, we also want to create a sense of connection between the young person and his or her culture. Recently I spent a month building a web site for our business. It was interesting. Page after page I moved through material thinking always of how it links up with other pages and layers. It seems a good metaphor for this storytelling initiation project.

We need to feel linked to the culture in which we find ourselves. We need to know the stories of family origins, community origins, national origins, and spiritual origins. We need to see how we fit in the larger "web" of the natural world. Knowledge and understanding of how we are linked creates a sense of cultural identity and personal security. Weak cultural links make us vulnerable to other influences like cults, gangs, scams, and powerful individuals. Weak links with our culture cause us to turn to subcultures to meet the need. Our need to find our connection to other people is a powerful force.

Stories enhance brain development. Sitting at the top of our sculls are ten billion brain cells waiting around for something to do. Stories encourage the brain to make pictures, to categorize and elaborate, to move and dance through the neural networks in a rich and life-enhancing way.

So, how do we tell a story that has the right stuff in it? How do we tell it in a way that will teach but does not preach? How do we make sure that it has a beginning, a middle, and an end? How do we measure the result on our listener's face without asking whether they *got* it? The following pages present a simple framework for story-telling. Much of it has been gleaned from the many years of practicing my own art as a storyteller both in print and on the radio. Study the framework in a general way and then forget about it. Let your stories come naturally and organically from your own experiences—but with a little bit of structure, thought, and intention.

Chapter Eight
Storytelling with Intention

A story is a simple little creature with a head, a body, and a tail. It can be very long or very short; it can be fat and move slowly or be slim and quick.

I was driving down the street, and on the far corner I saw a man standing. He had a gun. I turned left before the corner.

This is the shortest of short stories; a scene, a setting, a tiny sliver of conflict, and a conclusion. What if it began this way instead?

I was driving down the street, and on the far corner I saw a man standing. He had a gun in his right hand. His left hand was wrapped around the mouth of a small, terrified boy.

In the first example the logical choice was to turn left and seek safety. In the second story, the conflict is intensified and the moral dilemma heightened by the presence and danger of the small boy. Do we still turn left before we get to the corner? Do we abandon the child? Act like a coward? Seek help? What? What should we do? Drive forward, stop the car, get out and try to talk to the man? Go for the police? Each step takes us deeper into conflict, and the deeper the conflict, the more resourceful we have to become in order to resolve the conflict. This is the basic structure of a story.

I was driving down the road, and on the far corner was a man. He was holding the hand of a small, smiling boy. I drove by.

In this version of the same story we still have a beginning, middle, and an end but no conflict. Without conflict (the gun) the story becomes a passing observation.

A beginning, middle, and an end plus conflict equal a story. The teachers of writing tell us that there are really only three basic forms of conflict. This is probably true, however stories can become beautifully complex when a character engages in several of the following forms of conflict. The three forms of conflict are:

- Man versus Nature
- Man versus Himself
- Man versus Man

The male gender used here is for convenience only— the characters in our stories can be beasts, ants, humans, cows, pigs, men, or women. However, it is the inherently human qualities and situations that make us relate to a character whether it is one of the oddballs in the bar of Star Wars or a little piglet named Babe. This simple template helps to organize our minds around the stories that are stored in our own brains.

Man Versus Nature

In the "Man versus Nature" plot, conflict is presented by the natural world. Fire, wind, rain, flood, tornado, earthquake, frigid cold; all present ample conflict to one lone human or a group facing an emergency involving one of the forces of Mother Nature. Although the source of the conflict is in the external world, we are forced to seek inner resources. In native Hawaiian culture, the great legends and myths nearly all revolve around the heroes and Gods battling the raging sea, the angry typhoon, or the boiling volcano. The sweeter love stories speak of appeasing the natural forces with song and ritual to produce healthy crops. Their entire society circled around the natural forces of earth, sea, and sky.

This same form of conflict has spawned countless popular movies where a person or community must battle a blaze, survive an earthquake, or get safely to land. Inherent in this form of conflict is the need we have to find and use all available resources to overcome the crises. We need courage, endurance, fortitude, quick thinking, compassion etc. etc. A dangerous dance with the natural world brings these undiscovered personal characteristics and resources quickly to the surface.

When I was in college, my brother and two of his buddies took his new (used) little Chevy Nova out on the ice on Cass Lake, Minnesota, during the dead of winter. They were wheeling around, spinning cookies, and having a good time when suddenly the front tires found the soft ice caused by a warm, underwater current. The front end of the car dipped into the soft ice, and water rose around the front bumper. The boys moved fast. They threw open all doors and bailed out of the car. Once out of the car they had to move fast across the frozen lake in order to keep from getting frostbite or hypothermia. Quick choices took them to safety.

Later, the insurance man told them that the open doors were all that prevented the car from going down instantly. This is a simple story. Three guys wheeling around on a frozen lake: conflict—soft ice. A sudden activation of personal resources, fast thinking, and a quick hike across the lake. Safe once again.

It has all the elements of a story—a beginning, middle, end, and the sharp edge of conflict. Man versus Nature.

Man Versus Himself

The story conflict that engages "Man versus Himself" is perhaps, in truth, the only form of conflict because whether the battle is with nature or other people, it is always, ultimately, the discovery or development of our own character that will resolve these conflicts. Here, the subtle (or not so subtle) play of personal desires—jealousy, fear, anger, sadness—bring about conflict. We discover a character flaw or weakness and battle to overcome it in order to achieve some end. This is also perhaps the most powerful form of conflict that we have to deal with in initiating our young people. On the long road between childhood and adulthood, the individual must battle the inner, personal demons of fear, low self worth, selfishness, greed, cruelty, inadequacy, anger and on and on.

Luckily, we all have hundreds of our own personal stories that contain this element of conflict. And we have both the opportunity and responsibility to allow our young people to fight their own battles on this front. It is important here, as we explore the initiation of our young people, that we use our stories to assist them—but not do the work for them.

For example, once my 17-year-old daughter needed new contact lenses. I told her to call the doctor's office and make an appointment. It was interesting to watch the subtle play between us as she tried to get me to make the call for her. The conflict was minor—a twinge of fear—what do I say, how do I do it? She protects a part of herself from feeling foolish or inadequate. We all do. But in the end she made the call, made the appointment, and scored a small point for her Self. The conflict was not so powerful that it needed a story or intervention of any kind, but had I made the call for her, I would have scored the point—not her.

One of the great teachers in my life used to say "Never do anything for someone that they can do themselves." It's doing the hard thing, the right thing, doing what needs to be done when it needs to be done that puts us on the path to adulthood. Confronting inner fear and imagined failings allows us to do this. The larger the battle—the more ground we gain.

In my workshops and consulting practice, I see that fear is a deadly force that keeps us from going forward. It's as if we need to take on small fears over time—and overcome them—in order to get to a place where we can face the bigger fears.

When I was in college, I made a series of small traveling adventures before I attempted to fly overseas alone to attend school in Oxford for a half a year. Undertaking the earlier journeys prepared me for the bigger one—otherwise it would have been too much. Being a lifelong learner and creator *always* has fear as a part of its web and weave. We can't get along without it. When I first started speaking to groups, I was terrified and had to run to the bathroom several times before getting up to talk. Over time the fear got less and my speaking got better. They are partners, fear and accomplishment. If you are not afraid of the risk you are about to take—it probably isn't enough of a stretch.

Man Versus Man

The third form of conflict is "Man versus Man". Here, again, the conflict may come in the form of another individual or an entire army, but it is ultimately our own response to that *other entity* that builds character. This form of conflict is about relationships with other human beings. It is the common substance of the many spiritual teachings, fables, parables, and stories about how a human being should be with others.

In terms of adolescent initiation, we must consider what we want our young people to learn. What qualities and characteristics would serve them best throughout life? What strategies would we like them to develop? Do we want them to respond to conflict with other humans with sarcasm, fists, or guns? Or do we want them to respond with humanity, compassion, and courage?

When my son was eighteen and in his senior year, he would, of course, determine his own bedtime. My husband liked that last hour before bedtime alone so that we could talk and discuss the day. Often my son would park his long body in front of the gas fire and just lie there like a puppy. One night Milt just stopped talking, feeling a little resentful of the way Tom was in *our* private space. I kept talking, discussing the day, and asking questions as usual. Later I told Milt that I thought Tom was *studying* how relationships work. He's curious about how we do marriage. If we just shut down our "grown up talk" when he's around, how will he learn to do it?

All of the plot lines in "Man Versus Man" are relationship stories. The possibilities for conflict and tension between two people or groups of people are, of course, endless. One of the most common plots on the planet is boy meets girl, boy loses girl, boy finds a way to get girl back. Or the reverse; girl meets boy, etc. On a larger level, we have global conflict, ethnic dissidence, war, politics, etc.

In our storytelling paradigm, we need to find the personal stories that illustrate honest and effective ways of getting what we want, dealing with others, and taking care of relationship problems. There is no lack of material out there for us to draw on. Besides our own wellspring of personal stories, we can find good stories everywhere, from the Reader's Digest Magazine to the children's section of the local bookstore. We find small human-interest stories in newspapers, magazines, and on the radio that show one human being extending kindness, understanding, or courage in their dealings with others.

Unfortunately, on any given day we can find the horror stories, too, of those uninitiated, unaware human beings who know only brutality, cruelty, and lack of consciousness. It is so important that we carefully regulate the material entering the tender minds of our young people. This, too, is part of our job in initiating our young people. The young mind is as pliable as putty or Jell-o and cannot often discriminate between what is right and what simply is.

Even as we read these stories ourselves it causes something ancient and primal to rise up within us. Human beings want to reach for stars and spirit. They want to be larger than the life dictated by merely biological processes of shove it in, shove it out or blood endlessly circulating through a closed, tubular system. We long for spirit, heroes, bigger than life experiences, and the sacred.

Choosing a Point of View and a Voice

So, a story has a beginning, middle and an end. It engages one or more forms of conflict and the resolution of that conflict. A story also has a point of view or perspective. The most typical POVs for storytelling are to speak from the first person, third person, or omniscient perspective. In first person we use pronouns such as "I" and "me." It is my story and I am telling it to you. In third person, another tells the story and the pronouns used are "he" or "she". The omniscient point of view is bigger than first or third, as if God or the Creator was telling the story. Choosing a point of view for the stories that we want to tell changes the intimacy and voice of the story, as you can see in the examples below.

First person

I lived on Garden Circle, a half horseshoe of houses built by the mining company. My daddy worked in a taconite mine. Our little town was stuck in the middle of the wilderness in northern Minnesota. The trees were my best friends.

Third person

The little girl lived on a street called Garden Circle, which was built like a horseshoe with half circles of houses followed by more half circles. Everyday young fathers gathered on the street corners with battered black lunch boxes. They climbed on buses and were hauled off to the taconite mine up on the hill. The little girl missed her daddy.

Omniscient

   On the northern range of Minnesota a mining company moved into the quiet hillsides, ripping away trees and building roads. In 1953 they built a town. In 1954, they filled the town with young families of Swedish and Finnish descent who hadn't a clue what it would be like to belong to the company town.

If our goal is to tell stories that initiate, we may want to give fleeting thought to which point of view to use. First person is always suggested for our own personal stories. It is difficult sometimes to lay bare some of our painful or embarrassing stories which show us acting in foolish and sometimes dangerous ways. Parents, like myself, who were children of the sixties, might struggle with how much to reveal to their children of their own past. It's a difficult question that we should contemplate before we begin. Can our children benefit by knowing that we have smoked pot, shoplifted, or been caught doing all manner of crazy things? Can we clearly, as an adult, point out the faulty reasoning that was later corrected or honed by age and maturity? Can we reveal the hard things without losing our place as parent or somehow feeling that we are giving them permission to experiment with sex, drugs, and other dangerous or illicit behaviors? Each person must answer these questions individually. I do believe that we can get closer to the truth than many of us do. If we don't tell the stories, our children are asked to believe that we somehow sprung fully formed from our parents' heads. Without telling our stories, they'll think that we couldn't possibly understand their struggles and thus have no right to judge them—or guide them. Or they hear the lack of stories as a lie, a holding back of the truth.

The truth is that some of our greatest epiphanies come from the stupid and dangerous things we do. It's risky to share an intimate story that contains both our greatest weaknesses and our greatest strengths, but if we have integrated the learning we gained from having acted stupidly, we're bigger and stronger than we were before. I once realized that true personal strength comes when another person can find no weakness or flaws that I hadn't already discovered and examined in my own self. The soft spots in our character or personality are not due to our weaknesses—but to our *unexamined* weaknesses.

For example, after my first year of college I was longing for a larger world, a greater view than I'd had before. Signing up with a ride service at the University of Minnesota, I shared travel costs with two veterinary students traveling to Albuquerque, NM. To make a long and complex story short, I ended up living in a small house out in the valley with a bunch of dopers and hippies. One of the guys I'd met while his family was visiting Northern Minnesota two summers earlier. This life was definitely *widening* my perspectives. One girl was 8 months pregnant and every day this guy would come and give her heroin. She'd spend the rest of the day nodding and scratching. We had no money. I sold pints of blood plasma along with the winos and drunks for $5.00. Convinced that I'd found freedom and independence at last, I planted a garden, laid linoleum in the kitchen, and painted the walls. In odd juxtaposition to my surroundings, I spent lazy afternoons upstairs reading an old copy of *Little Women* by Louisa May Alcott that I'd borrowed from our landlord. It was cool—it was an illusion.

Then one night the guy I was with got so drunk that a bunch of his friends took him out on the front porch, hosed him down with the garden hose, and then threw him into bed fully clothed. The next morning he woke up and said, "How the f#%@ did I get all wet?"

Something in my mind snapped at that point. I remember the moment; the smell of the desert wind coming out of the valley, the smell of old beer on my new linoleum floor, the rapid death of my own illusions. For the first time I really looked again at my situation and knew exactly where it was leading. To jail—or the grave.

"Is this what I wanted?" I asked myself seriously. Is this what I dreamed of? Is this freedom and independence?"

Three days later, I caught a ride north with a cousin who took me home and back into college. This isn't one of my favorite personal stories. I was foolish and young. Later I could see that the beginning of my adventure— safely arranging a ride for myself, getting to Albuquerque, and making some efforts to live independently—were good things. The environment I placed myself into, however, was as bad as it could get. Fortunately, I made it out of there alive and without a criminal record.

I never told my mother that whole story, but I'll tell my children if I ever see them placing themselves into similar danger. And I'll tell the story in first person, claiming both the stupidity and the triumph, of getting into such a situation and then getting out again.

If, for some reason, we wish to tell the personal story as if it belonged to another, we could use third person. In the form of yoga that I practice, the teachers have a funny little character called Sheik N. The Sheik is a squirrelly little yogi who seems to learn all the lessons in the most haphazard and backwards way. In many Native stories there are characters called *contraries* that also seemed to do things in odd, backwards ways. In medieval societies there were jokers or court jesters to act out skits portraying the many stupid things that people do.

Many of these types of stories use humor to illustrate foolish behavior without naming names or pointing fingers—simply making the point. It's a gentle form of teaching. Even the cartoon, *The Family Circus,* has a fictional character called "Not Me" who gets into all sorts of troubles. In a family learning to use storytelling as a way to initiate and teach, we may want to create a make-believe relative who can't quite get the rules down and is forever stumbling into growth. "My Uncle Dim was the craziest sort . . . you know, one time Uncle Dim was walking down the road . . ." We could also create the family sage who always seems to have the best answer for things.

The omniscient point of view works best in large fables and fairy tales. In these stories the Gods, heroes, and great beings sit on the edge of the sky and see the big picture instead of just some tiny portion of it. I used this perspective in parts of a fairy tale I wrote in which *Makah*, Mother Earth, takes human form and joins her human family in order to put things straight again. The omniscient point of view sounds like this.

When darkness settled over the Black Hills and the outlying areas that night, the silence was peculiar—and pervasive. People found themselves whispering and turning down the television sets or turning them off completely. A great hush ruled the night.

Had even one had the eyes to see, they would have noticed that they were not alone but that pales wisps of light in pink and soft green and cream and pale orange—all the colors of the spectrum—had taken to the streets and alleyways and dirt roads of the numerous hills communities.

It was these night forms that insulated and absorbed, like pale pieces of cotton, all the busy, whirring images and sounds of a humanity lost to its own Self. Within their formless beings they carried tears and loss and drunkenness. They carried pain and memory. They moved like shock absorbers quickly between two souls bent on destroying one another. So, like humming street cleaners, these whisperers-in-the-night moved through a solid chunk of western South Dakota bringing about a completely silent, but irrevocable, revolution.

That excerpt is from a visionary novel entitled *One Drum*. It's one of my favorite omniscient passages because, when I imagine all those great spirits returning to these Black Hills, I feel somehow less alone as a human being. That's the goal of our storytelling—to create stories that make us feel connected, less alone, and able to go through the hard things toward something new.

Using the Right Tone of Voice

In addition to choosing the perspective or POV of your story, there are a few other things to keep in mind. One is to pay attention to the tone of voice and the words you emphasize in a story. This is an art. Alexander Pope in his *Essay on Criticism* suggested, "People should be taught, as if you taught them not." This is a good mantra to use for our storytelling activities. It's not our goal to use a story to club some poor child over the head with our *wisdom* and *knowledge*.

Here is a common sentence that opens many conversations. I write it four times here placing the emphasis on a different word each time. Say each one out loud in order to fully appreciate how the meaning changes with the specific word that is emphasized.

WHAT do you want?
What DO you want?
What do YOU want?
What do you WANT?

In the first question the tone implies impatience, aggressiveness, and perhaps even anger. In the second, it implies confusion, uncertainty, and many choices at hand. In the third the ball is in the hands of the one being asked. It also implies that perhaps I know what I want but do YOU? The fourth places the emphasis on the desire itself. WANT?

Of course there is a fifth attempt in which all words are evenly modulated and said smoothly with only a slight rise at the end. What do you want? Offering the question this way allows the person space, room to think, and a chance to answer.

In building our stories for initiation, we want to keep judgment, condemnation, hostility, frustration, and anger out. We want the story to unfold and be its own teaching tool without undue *author's message* hitting a person over the head.

It's amazing how powerful a tone of voice is. I remember a story one of my trainers told me about a girl who was attending college. She went to a desk in the front of the class and laid her books down just as the teacher was saying something to another person. Suddenly she slammed her books on the desk, snatched them back again, and stomped out of the room. Her reaction was triggered from the tone of voice the teacher was using with another student.

Many of our stories will begin with "When I was young . . ." and that's a good beginning. However, if every story begins with the righteous punch of *when I was young* (emphasis on 'I'), our young people will quickly learn to hear a lecture coming. *When I was a kid we didn't even have television . . . I had to walk fourteen miles to school in the snow, we didn't have cars or hot water . . . an outhouse out back*, etc.

Pay attention to tone of voice and modulation. Be sure to include many bits of sensory information; what a room smelled like, what the weather outside was that day, what the pine needles felt like beneath your feet, what the sound of the city was the day you were in the story. Use only enough detail to build the scene and not so much that it becomes boring and long.

The best indicator of the effectiveness of your stories is whether your listeners are interested from the beginning to the end? Do they stay with you? They will follow your story if you keep it honest, free of righteousness, and clear of the uncomfortable tonal qualities of a lecture or a sermon.

Telling the Right Stories at the Right Time

On my own long developmental path, I recall three lessons that helped me both as a human being, a therapist, and a writer. The first lesson was that we can only go as far with another person as we are willing to go ourselves. This lesson referred to my counseling work with others and said, basically, that I can't push a client to go into the dark corner that I myself have been unwilling to look into. This applies to parenting as well. We cannot ask our children to confront fears, habits, or behaviors that we are still secretly harboring ourselves. It becomes another example of do as I say—not as I do.

The second lesson I learned came from a book whose title and author I can't even recall (it was so many books ago). The author said that if you long for intimacy with another—give them your greatest intimacy. If you want a relationship to advance or deepen, you must give something of yourself in order to build trust and bonds. Relationships can only advance when there is trust and forward movement on the part of both partners. This also applies to spouses, children, and friends.

Finally, the third lesson came while I was doing a lot of public speaking and training. In this instance I was giving a couple's communication workshop for a group of campus wives at a local university. I'd been talking for maybe half an hour—espousing my greatest under-standings of how relationships really work. Finally, a young woman from the group threw out a comment that I heard, as "This is all easy for *you* to say." Her words stopped me cold. Without meaning to, I'd stepped up on a soapbox and was preaching to the masses. I didn't understand until later that teaching without a personal story is *always* preaching.

The impression that young woman got was not the one I wanted her to have. I stopped the lecture abruptly, and went and sat on her table, my legs dangling like a little girl. Instead of preaching, I told her stories of my long struggle with depression, of feeling alone in life, of yearning for relationships that fed me, and of my deep despair and sadness. The emotional atmosphere of the room changed instantly. Suddenly, I was *just one of them*, another woman who struggles, takes a few uncertain steps and maybe, just maybe, gains a little distance from my struggles.

I've never forgot that lesson. In any group I'm honored to speak to, I often test the emotional atmosphere. If the group is not as receptive as they could be—it's because I'm lecturing and not telling my own stories. Intellectual ideas mean more when backed by personal stories. People, young or old, do not like to be lectured to from on high.

Chapter Nine
How to Begin Storytelling

How do you know what story to tell—and when? A story is a good one when it is the right story at the right time. This sounds so simple until we consider the constantly changing kaleidoscope of our own child's development. From birth to death, the colors swirl and change, the desires shift as the brain juggles ten billion brain cells clamoring for attention. To keep it simple, we must train ourselves to better hear where our child is on a long developmental continuum.

For example, many of the manuals on sex education suggest that we only answer the questions asked and not offer too much beyond that. We let *their* curiosity and level of understanding dictate the amount of information given. This advice works here too. By observing our children, we can better understand whether their current struggles have to do with other children at school, a fear growing unattended in their middles, or a problem growing with procrastinating getting their schoolwork finished. By improving our ability to observe what is presented, we can match our stories to their current struggles at any age.

One day I was driving my five-year-old grand-daughter, Kayna, home after spending the night with us. We passed the elementary school where she would be starting Kindergarten that next fall. Everybody had been telling her how fun it will be, how exciting it was that she gets to go to school. When we passed the school, I saw her shudder a bit, and then rest her head on her arm with a forlorn look. It was clear that she didn't necessarily think it was *so exciting*. I told her a story.

"I remember my first day of school. We lived up in the north woods in Minnesota, about three blocks from the school. I had on new shoes, a new dress. My mother was going to let me walk to school all by myself."

Kayna was instantly interested. I went on. "It was so scary I thought I might pee my pants." Her head came up fast, and she giggled (like a five-year-old) at the thought of her grown-up grandma worrying about peeing her pants. And that famous food for a storyteller, the listener wanting to know what happened next, Kayna said, "Well, did you? Pee your pants?"

Slowly I told her how I had to push my toes to walk to school that day, all the time feeling scared with a tummy ache. And then I just had to march right into that school, go to my new room, meet that old teacher, and see those other kids. Then, and only then, did the fear go away—but by the end of the day I thought the teacher was nice and that school might just be a little fun.

A story? Little girl faces first day at school. Feels great fear. Conquers fear and goes anyway. Discovers school is going to be okay.

This is a story that every adult and school age child in America shares. In fact, when I was telling my husband, Milt, about it later he sheepishly told me the story of how his mother had to take him back to the classroom three times because he kept leaving. One story has a way of reawakening stories in others. That is another thing to remember as we consider which stories to tell. Often the right story will simply arise naturally from the cauldron of our own memories. When this happens, give only fleeting consideration to the structure and details of the story to be sure it includes the right stuff. In fact, here is a quick template (a reminder of the earlier info) to use for judging whether a story meets the well-formed criteria. A story has:

- a beginning, a middle, and an end,
- one or more forms of conflict,
- matches the age and developmental level
  of the child,
- has an effective point of view and tone of voice,
- is told with intention and with honesty,
- and outlines the steps to discovery (strategies
  used for solving the conflict)

Naturally, these rules can be broken. There'll be many occasions when a small sketch or vignette will do in place of a story. These are like small chunks of stories or brief character descriptions. This material is like the filler between all your other stories.

Telling a Story with Intention

Intention is the difference between an aimless ramble down a city street versus walking to make an appointment on time. A story with intention has a destination and a way of getting there. Stories that are told with intention have a greater chance of hitting their mark. Our goal, ultimately, is to make use of stories in a natural and organic way to present our understanding of the way life works.

However, especially to begin with, we might think a story through to determine its power points, the internal structure, and our goal in telling it. We have to be aware of too much obsessive detail—it kills a good story. We've all known people whose stories seemed to ramble on and on without a single relevant point or a satisfactory ending. This form of storytelling is simply boring. In fact, many movies and books suffer from this same problem.

What is the reason or intention in telling the story? The intention of a story will fall somewhere within four basic, generalized story types. The first type contains the stories that connect us with our own family, community and history. The second type contains the stories that teach and illustrate useful strategies for living. A third and higher form suggests to the child that there is more to life than that we have to pay taxes and die. This story type points the child toward a future vision and a reach toward higher spiritual structures. The fourth type is interactive and includes stories that the child will tell us thus setting up a two-way flow of stories.

Stories that connect

A healthy adult feels connected to family, to the ancestral lineage, and to the community in which he or she lives. Many stories can be told for no other reason than to build small bridges of communication between parents and children. These stories include a lot of humor, entertaining family stories, stories about the child's birth and early years, stories about our own childhood, the funny things we did, the ways we entertained ourselves etc.

Children can be invited to tell their own stories about school, what the teacher did, what their friends did etc. These stories should be woven throughout every single day in great abundance. Although they may not fit all the above criteria for what a story is, it doesn't matter. Our goal or intention in this layer of storytelling is to keep all lines of communication open and flowing freely. Instead of "What did you do in school today?" where you get the classic response of "Nothing," ask instead, "What was the funniest thing that happened today? Were there any monsters in school today? Did the teacher tell any stories?"

With smaller children we can even get into more make believe stories that encourage imagination and creativity. We can ask them what they would have done if a large, slimy slug oozed into the classroom and tried to sit at a desk and would it have made the students laugh because he kept sliding off the chair again? Make this storytelling a fun, loose, and creative time. Besides being entertaining and fun, we can also remember that pushing the mind for the non-ordinary answers builds more and more neural connectors in the brain.

Once I asked my son (he was about eight) the following question. "If you had lived another lifetime in another place, what would it have been?" I was stunned when he went into this long story about living in Russia, seeing the dirt roads, wearing rugged clothes, and sometimes dreaming in Russian. He said his name was "Capiune." I've no idea what any of it meant—but he was as clear as a bell about it all.

A healthy adult feels connected to his or her community and culture. Some stories dip into family history and roots. They can include the stories about how great grandfather came from Norway, or how Grandma used to cook in a logging camp in the north woods, or how old Uncle George watched his barn blow away in a Kansas tornado. We can think in terms of both ethnic roots and actual family histories. Some of the stories may not seem to have much conflict but are like small human interest stories about the family that your children have both a right and a need to know. Recent Internet research indicates that the most visited web sites (after porn) are family genealogy sites. The huge interest in genealogy research underscores the fact that we hunger for family stories. I read a story once about a white woman who decided to look into family roots only to discover that her great grandmother was the first black woman to graduate from an eastern college. The woman didn't know she had an African American grandmother.

Hearing the stories that put us in this place at this time strengthens our cultural or social identity. We didn't simply land in this country, region, or neighborhood. A series of historical events brought us to this time and place. In ancient, tribal cultures there were no written histories and everything was given orally. Even today in some tribes the family stories and songs are considered family property. A family valued its songs and stories as some of its most prized possessions.

The stories were the only way to build a series of links from the present into the distant past. Without the stories, this information would be lost. We in the modern world have not forgotten this need to be linked to our past—we feel it deeply within. Even today lost letters or diaries that surface belonging to important historical figures or our own family members are highly treasured. We long to hear of their experiences, what they went through in order to survive, what carried them through the mysterious loops of time.

When I was a very young girl, my great-grandfather was in his nineties. All I really knew about him was that he smelled of old tobacco and always had a ready supply of lemon drops to pop into our mouths when we visited him. He lived in a small apartment next to my grandmother's house. Once I saw an old trunk that held a lamp and had writing on it. I asked Grandmother about it and she said Great Grandfather had carried that old wooden trunk out of Denmark when he immigrated. I was too young then to ask him any questions. I cared only about lemon drops and his bouncing knee.

I still know nothing about his journey from Denmark or even where in Denmark he came from. How old was he? Who did he leave behind? How did he manage it? As a young girl I considered only that he was, and always had been, an old, old man. Now the questions come and there is nobody left to ask. When we visited Hellinger in Austria, he told us that Americans are restless because they seek their relatives.

When family storytelling has become a common element in our daily lives, we might even want to take a recorder to still-living elders and grandparents, sit with them, and ask them to tell stories. We can ask them about how they lived, what changes they have seen, how they cooked, what they did before television, etc. Dig out old family pictures and ask the elders who the people in the pictures are and what they did. Although America really is a melting pot with a population that constantly shifts locations, we all came from somewhere. Even the tribal groups traveled across the lands.

Creating links and a sense of connection is the key to this layer of storytelling. Without these we feel alienated and alone. Depression, isolation, and despair are on the rise both in our younger population and the general population. Could it be the lack of relevant and meaningful stories?

Building curiosity about our neighborhoods and communities is also an important part of adolescent initiation. With events such as the horrible mass murder of students in Littleton, Colorado and other communities, we can't help but assume those young people had no sense of belonging or affection for their community or school. It was a terrible missing piece, and most of are terrified about what it says about us as a society. We feel helpless, unable to name the villain here. We long to be part of the solution but find ourselves caught in endless bouts of useless analysis. Using a storytelling approach to create curiosity about our immediate community could be a small part of the solution. By turning backwards in time to one of the most consistent and ancient forms of communication—storytelling—we may be able to make our tribe strong once again.

When I began this project many years ago, I impulsively joined two police officers at a table in our local Happy Chef and asked them what they thought about youth in this community. I explained what I was working on and asked their opinion. It was interesting: their analysis had to do with the lack of communication between neighbors. One officer said that he constantly answers calls about kid problems in a neighborhood that, at one time, the neighbors themselves would have dealt with. If a kid throws an egg at your house, you march over to that kid's house and tell his parents to deal with the kid. Now, the officer said, the offended parent calls the police.

It's possible to even extend this storytelling approach into neighborhoods in order to make more direct links with one another. What do you know about the stories of your neighbors? Do you know where they came from, what work they do, what their favorite movies and activities are?

Stories that teach

A young person must learn the steps needed to develop successful strategies for living. This kind of storytelling relates most directly to initiation practices for our young people. We need to find ways to impart important information and strategies without carrying a baseball bat or lecturing endlessly. Here the story we tell will contain a direct lesson and the steps we took to achieve a desired outcome. Here, in particular, we must be careful of the tone of voice and the right telling of the story. Our intention is to tell a story in such a way that it naturally fits the reality of the young person, and they are able to relate it in some way to their own experiences.

Telling stories is not meant to *replace* the need for steady discipline or explaining what rules. Rather, it is a rich *addition* to spouting household rules. It's a way to place the rules in the larger context of the family.

Milton Erickson, well known for his work in hypnotherapy, used stories constantly to enrich lives and change old patterns. As he heard a person's problem, he would place it in the "class of problems" stored in his mind. Next he would slide over and consider the "class of solutions" and pick an appropriate story from that class to help resolve the problem. For instance, to a child who is wetting the bed he may tell stories of how a baseball player must *control* the bat, *clenching his muscles* in just the right way, waiting for the *right moment* to release his hold. This is what we can do with our stories. We hear the problem from our child and then find the appropriate story that contains a solution. His use of metaphors was masterful and took years to develop. Our stories do not need to be subliminal to be effective.

We can use our own stories or turn to the thousands of teaching stories available in every corner of the world. These stories sort themselves out in a wide variety of ways but all have the goal of imparting information about relationships with the self, others, money, community, school, and the spiritual world. Below are brief descriptions of the many types of stories that fall under the category of teaching stories. These are just a few.

Hero stories: These stories tell of a character who overcomes great adversity or giant obstacles to obtain a goal. The characters may be mythical gods, prairie wives, Indian chiefs, beasts, sports heroes, or career giants. In fact, we find heroes in every walk of life and down every historical trail. Whether they are children or Gods, they can still be heroes.

The power of these stories comes from a person, just like you or me, reaching high above his or her personal obstacles to reach and obtain a goal. The bottom line is that we all want to have a hero or be a hero.

Value Stories: Value stories are about people using human kindness, honesty, integrity, fairness, justice, etc. as an approach to problems and life. In a value story, the obstacle to be overcome usually is a hidden one such as selfishness or greed. A child has two suckers and meets a friend on the sidewalk. Does he give the second sucker to the friend or stick them both in his pocket and save them for later?

Telling stories with value themes is a way to indicate to young people that they are linked to a larger community and must always consider that community. The Hopi story of offering water to the young corn plants before drinking any himself is an example of this story type.

Quality of character: These stories are similar to value stories but are more sharply focused on what kind of personal qualities we wish to acquire in life. How do we want others to see us? One of my favorite stories in this category is the one about the couple that is moving to town and they meet an old man sitting on a porch and ask him what kind of town this is. The man asks what their last town was like, and the couple tells one nasty story after another about how cruel and selfish the people were. When they finish the old man says, "Yep, that is just what this town is like." Another couple comes along and asks the same question and the old man asks again what their last town was like. This time the couple is full of praise about what a wonderful, generous, beautiful place their old town was. The old man says, "Yep, that's what this town is like."

Attitudes toward the world and other people greatly influence whether our experience of life is great—or lousy. Quality of character stories emphasize strength, a positive attitude, courage, and selflessness.

Prosperity and work stories: Young people are very concerned about making correct career choices. They want to find work that satisfies and pays them well at the same time. (Actually many adults are in the same boat.) My favorite stories of this type feature a person who strongly believes in something even when it looks impossible. He or she moves ahead and is highly successful—the rags to riches story.

We can find many true stories of this kind in the biographies of great scientists, teachers, inventors, and public leaders. There are also many wonderful books in the self-help/motivation section of the bookstore with this theme. It is my personal belief that these stories encourage young people to look outside the normal paradigm of grades/college/high paying job and to find their own unique dream. The present world offers numerous opportunities for an entrepreneurial approach to making a living. We could also encourage them to value self-satisfaction as much as the paycheck that comes with work.

Teacher stories. Some of the most beautiful stories include the timely arrival of a teacher at those difficult moments in life. Teacher stories acknowledge those sweet souls who stepped in and helped us when we most needed help. As we scan our own stories, we will find a teacher, a kind neighbor, friend, coach, stranger, or boss who somehow saw our need and filled it. We must always acknowledge our teachers in the stories we tell. These stories can also emphasize that no matter where we are in our lives, we will always be a "student" in need of a teacher.

Mystical stories: It isn't enough to simply introduce our children to the *facts* of life. Mystical stories encourage us to lift our eyes to the higher realms and explore such mysterious concepts as imagination, spirit, philosophy, God, and finding our right place in the universe. Children are always and naturally interested in the supernatural worlds as well as this world. Although many parents fear this unknown themselves, it is important to allow for exploration of the other realms.

The careful separation of church and state has disallowed such philosophical exploration in the school systems, so we must satisfy this need by providing a rich source of stories in which the characters take on the mysterious unknown. We could note the giant popularity of the Harry Potter books as evidence of this need. The fascination with strange, weird movies and books is a strong indication of the strength of this interest in young people. Be careful not to let *Hollyweird* guide your child into the dark side of the unknown.

Future-vision stories: In many years of working with others, I find that depression and sadness often come because we cannot see beyond this moment—we have no vision of the future. Future vision stories can be used like a game within the family to encourage children to look out and beyond this moment. We can entertain the most outrageous futures and perhaps, in the process, find the vision that actually excites us. Once I did a group ice-breaker by asking each member to say what was the most outrageous thing they could imagine doing. By the time the group was finished, each person was a little more in touch with what they really wanted—and that their requests were not so far out.

Who do you want to be when you grow up? What is the vision you have of your life? There are many great examples out there in the sports and motivational books for the power of visualization for creating change and better strategies for life. I cannot over-emphasize the power of these mental phenomena. I once had a client who felt like he was going nowhere fast, so in a session I asked him to pretend that ALL obstacles had been removed and he could have, be, or do whatever he wanted to do in the world. I let him think about it a minute and then asked him "Now, what do you most want?"

He looked at me and said, "I'd really like some camping gear, maybe a tent and a sleeping bag." His future vision was pretty small. In fact, it barely reached past his nose. Many of us believe that a person is more likely to make right choices in life if they have a long-range view or sense of themselves in mind. Find stories that illustrate this.

Making our Fortune: This type of story highlights our desire for independence and becoming our own person. We could also call them quest stories. The young one goes off to seek his fortune and comes back having fulfilled the quest. As you can tell, there is a lot of overlap in these simple categories of stories. I lay this one out as separate because in the "making our fortune" type of story, we also long for that acknowledgement by our community that yes, we have actually come back with our fortune. This is, basically, a rite of passage or initiation story.

Romance stories: After finding the right career, perhaps one of the primary concerns of young people is making the right choices in finding a life partner. These stories take us to the realm of the heart—finding our life mate, creating rich relationships, and having regard, love, and a rich personal romance. Be careful not to present only the Cinderella, happily-ever-after romances. As much as we all wish it were like that, we need to learn many, many strategies for having successful relationships. These stories also contain many values and future vision stories and should encourage our young to be true to who they are within their relationships. Share your own stories about how you found your partner and what it really takes to keep love alive.

Case studies and self-help books can be a good source of stories that outline the many careful steps that we must (or must not) take in order to build solid personal partnerships. These can also be helpful. We have all picked up psychology books and scanned the pages looking for the examples that parallel what we ourselves are experiencing.

There are probably many story types I've forgotten, but what is important to remember is that we want to think ahead so that we match our storytelling to the constantly unfolding development of our young people. Again, a *good* story is the right story at the right time. It's important for children to see the process by which their elders came to be Elders. Stories that relate most directly to their current experiences are the best. When Kayna was afraid of her first day of school, I didn't turn to her and say, "Don't be afraid. There is nothing to be scared of." That isn't good enough. The brain doesn't understand the word *don't*. It needs specific examples and explanation. No, instead I joined her reality with a story of my own fear of my first day at school. I showed her how I overcame my fear—and did not wet my pants.

The best parent/storyteller will be the one who has thought through his or her stories carefully and can present them in complete packages. This means not conveniently editing out the hard or embarrassing parts of the difficult process that brought the story to a conclusion. This does not mean that our stories must always have a happy ending. One of the hard facts of life is that it sometimes takes us decades to learn from a single bad choice. Better to tell the truth. In truth, we would all like our children to be able to skip over the long, hard parts of gaining maturity but this robs them of being able to discover the texture and weave of their own life fabric.

On another note, we must also limit our stories if they will somehow burden the child. During a recent showing of our film, *Video Letters from Prison*, an ex-prisoner said that he realized he must not pass his own pain onto his children. That pain he must carry alone.

Hostile Storytelling

Finally, there is one note I want to make here about what constitutes bad storytelling. Bad storytelling is hostile, told only to humiliate, poke fun at, dump guilt on, or put our own heads above another's. We do not tell stories to lift ourselves above others and show how smart we are to the *dumb* listener. A good story lifts—it does not degrade. Likewise, when a child or young person tells you one of their stories, take it as a gift. Never use it against them at a later time. Telling stories requires an atmosphere of trust and respect that enriches the soil for future storytelling.

Poking fun at, teasing, or embarrassing a child with stories is an acceptable use of the story. One of the most destructive forces in any family is this use of what I call *hostile humor*. Hostile humor often masks all the unspoken resentments and hurts of a family's daily life. When communication isn't possible, we turn to hostile humor and then deepen the destruction by saying "What? Can't you take a little joke?"

Don't turn to hostile humor as a way of calling out flaws and faults. If you hear it done between brothers and sisters, call them on it immediately. If you see children in the neighborhood picking on one other child, stop them instantly. We cannot condone this behavior. If there is a show on the television that pretends that sarcasm, ridicule, or violence is funny, shut it off now. If a movie or program doesn't tell stories that match the values and strategies that you want your child to have, then push the power button to off. We have far more control over what goes in than over what comes out later.

The truth is, bad stories are everywhere and one of the most important jobs as a parent is to monitor the flow of junk material into the child's brain until he or she is able to learn discrimination. We monitor the noxious gases in our homes, the exhaust system of our cars, the foods that go in, the language we use—and yet we do not monitor the material that is fed daily into the unsuspecting young brain. Beware of bad storytelling.

What are my stories?

At first we may think that we have few stories, that our stories are not too interesting, or that our life has been dull. However, if we look a little closely, we'll find stories in the most unlikely and easily overlooked places. I remember reading a book once where the author suggested I walk through my house and see where I could find "me" in the house. The exercise was quite informative. In fact, I finally found "me" in a small box of letters and trinkets from my youth, and in one single picture hanging on my wall. It seemed sad that I could find none of myself there in my own home.

Today, my house is full of my stories. Beneath my pretty gas fireplace is a wooden platform filled with the rocks I collected from the many bodies of water and far away places we have visited: quartz, river rock, slate, granite, sandstone bowls with small balls inside of them. I remember the story behind most of the rocks and have written Rio Grande or Lake Superior on the bottoms of others. I love those stony stories beneath the source of warmth in my house.

A story can be simply the time I cranked the car window down and suddenly felt the air on my face and knew I was *awake*. A story can be in one small finger of my newborn baby as she reaches for empty air.

If you like to write, take a pen and start writing. If you like to carry a little hand-held recorder, tell your stories on tape. These are your stories and it's likely that many of them match the experiences your child or children are going through right now. Natalie Goldberg, author of *Writing Down The Bones*, suggests we do ten minute timed writings that begin with opening statements. "What I remember most about . . . the kitchen of the house I grew up in, or the first day of school . . ." Write until the words run out and then begin again with, "What I most *don't want* to remember about the kitchen, the first day . . ." You don't have to be a "good" writer to engage memory this way—and you will be amazed at what flows out of your pen.

To assist in finding stories in our lives, here is a list of suggestions for scanning personal experiences for stories. This is another list but, as you read it, stories will come hopping out of the bushes like bunnies. Capture them and take a look. See what pulses there, what lessons were learned. Remember the sounds, smells, and sensations that went with the story.

First experience with: Death, starting school, finding your best friend, beginning a romance, sex, alcohol, drugs, first job, fight, menstrual period, major achievement, win, getting in trouble, realization of something, being a new kid in school, solo drive, encounter with danger, philosophical thought, good idea, hunting experience, competition with others, humiliating experience.

Personal Demons: Personal encounters with fear, lust, jealousy, anger, greed, rage, violence, sadness, despair, depression, etc.

Encountering our inner demons successfully moves us from one life stage to another. We can't build soul and strength without taking them on face to face. These negative experiences, when met forcefully, provide powerful turning points that allow us to shift direction toward the life we most want.

Gods and Great thoughts: Encounters with joy, extrasensory experience, awareness of the universe, awareness of spiritual world, ghosts, mysteries, strange moments, déjà vu', great teachings, great souls, synch-ronicity, and religious experience.

There is a reason that young children on up through adolescence are enamored with ghost stories, time travel, aliens, and outer space. They long for a wider awareness of how the universe works. They want mystery and magic. Just recently I was scanning the books available in the youth section of the local bookstore. Fully half to three quarters of the book had something to do with space or the supernatural. We can fear this trend—or we can understand the intrigue and meet it.

Events: Car accidents, moments of danger or greatness, birth of a child, a new home, approval from a parent, graduations, proms, being trusted with a specific task, meeting your mate, marriage, entering college, travels, meeting a teacher, events of child's life, etc.

Sometimes from our greatest hardships comes the greatest leap of development. We can share these stories with our children, and recognize the potential when they face their own difficult events.

Stories that surround questions: What is the meaning of life? How big is the universe? Why is there war? What does it feel like to die? Will I like being an adult? Why does he treat me that way? How does a chicken cross the road? Why are we killing the earth? What do we need money for? Why can't I live in a hut in the woods and be left alone?

It has been my experience with my children that they love to examine stories that push their understanding beyond known limits. Kids want to know. They hunger to know even when there are no answers. Like an empty belly, we can feed this other belly with stories and questions.

Stories that pose situational ethics: What would you do in this instance? Four people are on a deserted lifeboat but there is only food and water for three. What do you do? A person is caught in a burning building and there are only moments to act—you are the only one there. You find a million dollars in a bag on the side of the road. What do you do with it? Your aging mother/grandmother is slowly dying from a terrible disease—and she asks you to end her life. What do you do?

Posing these questions to children pushes them to scan their values and beliefs in a discovery process. They may have strong ideas but not realize it. Posing situational moral questions such as these brings a lively exchange and offers the opportunity for other stories.

Historical Stories: Historical stories place us in time, and give us identity. This may include stories about the family, the ancestors, the homelands, the community in which we live etc. Where did our family come from? How did we get here? What events have had a powerful effect on us? What was grandmother like, grandfather like? What did they do for a living?

Children may not realize that they hunger for these stories until, like me, with my great grandfather and my mother, it was too late. I found so little when my mother died and didn't realize how much I wanted to know about her. Gather the stories while you can.

This list, again, is incomplete, intended only to stir the pot of our own memories for possible stories that could be used in the initiation and teaching of our young people. They want to know our stories. The younger our children are when we begin telling the stories, the firmer our lines of communication will be. They'll find our stories more engaging, more interesting, and more relevant than a video game or a television program.

Chapter Ten
Creating the Story Time

The beauty of this simple story approach is that it has the ability to increase family intimacy and strength, *and* initiate the young adult. A story is like a drink of water, easy to find and so satisfying. However, even a quick little story requires a certain set of environmental conditions. It requires time. It requires that we be present in our own mind to the story being told, and 100% present to the one we are telling it to. This, for many, will require subtle shifts in the daily patterns of our family life. We have to build the right atmosphere for stories to happen. We no longer have the many hours of winter darkness where we can sit before a warm, roaring fire and tell stories. The electric light bulb obliterated those hours, and extended our workday. The modern world has since slowly wiped out nearly all opportunities for stories to happen. We need to forcibly take back that time.

Many families are so intent on providing their young people with the right *opportunities* to develop that we miss this oh-so-important factor of time spent together. Young families are stressed trying to meet the many demands of an overburdened family schedule. They must run off to the soccer games, ballet lessons, school conferences, dental appointments, and football games. They race home, and madly try to slap a meal together to stuff the empty bellies before bath and bed. They do this dance often with two parents working full time, earning money, paying taxes, and putting clean laundry in the drawers. We've all become master jugglers in this circus of modern life, and yet we're starved for the solitude and silence needed to restore both mind and body for another day at the circus.

When I was teaching NLP, I used to give groups a simple assignment. Imagine each morning a little genie appears at your bedside with ten quarts of energy—your allotment for the day. Just ten quarts! Then I'd ask them to analyze how they generally use their ten quarts throughout the day. It was always a shocking exercise. Most find that, in spite of the limited ten quarts, they've tried to magically use fifteen or twenty quarts. They end each day by falling into a deathly slumber that is more like running out of gas then restful sleep.

Scanning our lives in a realistic and honest way is a difficult thing. However, the truth is that we have little, or nothing, to offer anybody if we've used our ten quarts up by noon every day. Making small lifestyle changes can be the beginning of creating a new and useful environment within the home for stories to happen.

The first change is to dump all activities that no longer fit or serve who you are today. The second is to dump as much *stuff* as you can to reduce the endless use of energy needed to pick up stuff, move stuff from one place to another, pile stuff here, pile stuff there, wash stuff, etc. Think Japanese. Think tipi. Think gypsy wagon. Think cave. Get rid of the junk. Use less, want less, and take less. If you have fourteen appliances for dicing and slicing, dump them all and buy a single sharp knife.

On one of our collection trips to a small village in Mexico, the simple and beautiful huts of the villagers stunned me. There was no excess garbage or junk lying around that wasn't in use. I realize that poverty is not the answer to the overload of our society—and yet I came home feeling like a bloated, over-junked American gringo.

Next, learn to *just say no*. We had this crazy and useless campaign trying to teach our young people to just say no to drugs when many of us haven't a clue how to say no to anything ourselves. We serve on committees, talk on the phone, take care of other people's responsibilities, max out our credit cards, and generally abuse our bodies with junk food and negative thoughts because we haven't learned to just say no. How are we supposed to teach our children this if we haven't learned it ourselves?

Having smoothly accomplished these few, little lifestyle changes (yes, I smile), there are even more elegant ways to introduce storytelling into your family. Here are just a few suggestions about how to create ripe opportunities for storytelling. Better yet, turn them into regular family rituals.

- Do chores *together*, such as dishwashing and clothes folding.
- Use time spent in the car while crossing town to appointments to tell stories.
- Skip the movie you were going to rent and try silence—the natural moment before a story.
- Go on short adventures in the car that requires only an hour or two to a local fun place. Time in the car, again, is a good time for stories.
- Throw out the television. Or turn it off. Or put it in a room away from the *living* room.
- Sign up for fewer activities. Quit others.
- Cook supper together as a family.
- Take walks together.
- Make an evening place to sit out under the stars together
- Take breaks. Take your son or daughter alone with you to a local café and have a coke or a hot chocolate.
- Do yard work together.
- Develop the Fifteen Precious Minutes before bed habit to ask for stories.

- Read stories.
- Grow a garden.

You notice how many of the suggestions above contain the word *together*. We can only find relief from isolation *together*. I know you will find many other opportunities besides these to tell stories. The key is to quit requiring family members to do household tasks in isolation as *dreadful chores* that must be done. Remember, we want them to learn to be *contributors* and not just *consumers*. We want to take our place as parent and not police enforcer. We can overcome the little wiggle of fear that comes when we suddenly find ourselves in a room with others and *there is no distraction*. Stories will naturally weave themselves around the other activities of our day if we allow them. Once we begin, we'll find that our young people will seek us out for more of this rich time.

Finally, build stories together. Stories that we share with others are like golden threads that link us forever with another person or group. Over time the individual experiences and stories will weave a web of pure gold. As a family it's important to be constantly creating and expanding the realm of shared stories. For instance, if you are a man and have a son and have taken that son (or daughter) through his initiation into hunting, that cache of stories will perhaps be central to the relationship that you have with your son. In many families the first hunt is still as important as the hunting initiation conducted in families a thousand years ago. There is something primal and central to our history here and it becomes an important story in our shared history. However, we want to be constantly expanding the realm of stories so that the entire relationship does not rest on that one cache of stories.

I've met so many people who constantly cycle back to one story as if they have not progressed. Stories about life on the street, the sixties, hunting, veterans or comrades in war, disaster victims, basketball buddies, the high school prom queen, or being abused as a child are examples. We've all been to that class reunion or met that old friend and felt that first burst of *remember when* only to have it die out rather abruptly because all we have in common is that one set of stories. It's odd how one powerful story can make all other stories pale. Life is a collection of stories—not one single story.

Beware of being locked into one particular triumph or terror and not building stories beyond that. Be very careful that your own life has not become organized around one story, perhaps an alcoholic parent, an incest event, a rape, car accident, or other personal tragedy. As painful as the story may have been, you can't allow it to control all other stories from that point forward. This is a difficult thing to get. The opposite side of this coin is letting your life be controlled by a single triumph, perhaps the time you became Miss South Dakota, or the time you won the State A basketball game for your team. Life is about gathering many, many stories. Imagine being forced to read the same book every day for the rest of your life, over and over again. You'd be bored to tears by the end of the first week.

The primary relationships in our families and lives should have many, many pockets of stories to draw on, creating a complex and beautifully formed web of connections that bind us to one another. Recently, I had the idea to skim through my journals and fragments of stories and to put together an "I remember" book for my siblings. It occurs to me that we could also do this in a round robin approach, and I could ask them to send me their "I remember" stories to add to the book over time. Such a book would be a treasure to any family. Since our parents died, my seven siblings and I have made an effort to gather at every Thanksgiving. Guess what we do during those precious days (besides eat)? We tell stories.

.

The Universal Separation Story

Assume now that we have told the stories. Even before reading this book we've been telling stories. They're a natural part of life. We have begun telling stories with more consciousness and intention. Our stories have now grown into a complex web of life stories that we've created with our child over many years. In addition to the stories (or through them), we've taught the child to drive a car, manage a checkbook, analyze their emotions, wash their own clothes, cook, and survive the first job interview. We've hovered over them as they learned A, B, C, and 1, 2, 3. Each accomplishment, each developmental step has been watched, tested, and completed. Now, at last, we come again to that place that I've spent ten years trying to figure out.

How do we complete their initiation? How do we launch them from this nest that we've sheltered them in for so long? How do we finally pluck the ripe fruit of this long task of parenting and see them into adulthood?

The Big Woods

I spent my early childhood up in the north woods of Minnesota, nearly in Canada. My father worked for Reserve Mining and the small mining town was filled with young parents and small children. We played in packs like wolves or dogs. Near our house there was what we called "the little woods," a small muddy stream, and then "the big woods" beyond. Occasionally we would challenge one another to stray off into the big woods but none of us ever got very far. We knew that in the big woods a small child could get lost—separated forever from home, mom, dad, and safety. Beyond that small stream were all the large and scary things. Our fear was great.

One of our greatest human fears is to be lost and separated from home—and yet the separation story is one of the most powerful stories of all time. We fear separation from those we love or that which we know and are familiar with. We recognize at some instinctual and very elemental level that our safety is dependent upon the good will of others. In many native or ancient cultures, the ultimate punishment was to be exiled and sent away. In those cultures, exile often meant death. In today's high school, one of the greatest fears is to be outcast and ostracized by our peers.

Tarzan, The Wizard of OZ, the story of Moses, *The Clan of the Cave Bear, The Lord of the Flies, Hansel and Gretel,* there is an endless list of stories and books in which the central conflict is separation from what we know. Charles Dickens literally supported himself by ripping small young children from their parents in his stories.

Separation stories are universal, an integral part of initiation and the rite of passage for young people. Contained within this fear is the possibility for our greatest triumph—to master the fear. When we master the fear we discover that we can make it alone and find ourselves linked to an even greater familial and spiritual connection.

In almost equal proportion are the separation stories in which the young person chooses or is directed to separate from his world in order to become an adult. Consider Hercules, Jesus in the desert, the Three Little Pigs, Jason and the Argonauts, and Siddhartha. From cultures around the world, this separation story is told. A youth must leave the home of his or her parents to go on quest that is universal in nature.

During my college years I made the decision to go and study in Oxford, England for two trimesters. In order to get to that point I had to save the money, sign the papers, get a passport, purchase insurance, and arrange a million small details. Finally, I was ready. I'd tried (somewhat desperately) to find others to join me but ended up going alone. The day I left is still etched clearly in my mind. My parents took me to the airport, followed me down the long hallway and through security. At that point I was sure they would follow me straight out to the plane and take seats on either side of me.

At departure time, my mother and father stood in a window and watched me walk out across the tarmac on the first steps of my journey. I can't know exactly what they felt, but I felt as though I was trying to swallow an orange whole. Inside I was terrified, excited, confused, wanting to turn back, wanting to go forward—but I got on the plane, fastened my seat belt, and flew away. Six months later, I returned a different person.

During that trip I rode the trains across Europe during our trimester break. At one point I found myself on a train platform in Switzerland standing before a large schedule board with all the great cities of Europe on it. I'd separated from my travel companions earlier with plans to meet up again in Venice. With a Europass in my hip pocket, I could choose any destination; Rome, Paris, Madrid, Barcelona . . . I felt huge, and alone. It was exhilarating.

I had separated and become a part of something larger.

Consider your own history. What was that moment for you? At what point did you know that you were no longer tethered to mom and dad but alone, separate, and free to make your own choices? The moment might have been a dramatic separation like my trip to Europe or a less dramatic, but still profound, moment when you realized that your life was your own to do with as you wish. I'd be interested in hearing your stories. I'm collecting them for research and later use, so send me your story.

Chapter Eleven
What is an Elder-Based Culture?

Throughout this book I've made frequent references to our need to return to an Elder-based culture. It occurs to me now, at the end of this writing journey, that I haven't actually defined that clearly for you or myself. Elder-based culture—it certainly sounds good, but what does it mean?

On the surface, the meaning is obvious. Elders are the old ones, the members of our families and communities who have already passed through most of the life stages except one—death. In smaller traditional native communities the Elders have real status. Our experience in Indian country bears witness to this. The Elders are given first voice on issues. The children of the community are taught to bring food and drink to the Elders at any gathering before taking what they want. Elders are consulted on important policy issues and mediate conflict between younger tribal members. When we look again at mainstream American society, this status is not so apparent. Oddly, like our youth, the Elders have lost their rightful place in the world.

In the current culture, the Elders have become *Elderly*, often seen as frail, sickly, unable to contribute, and a burden on society and their families. This is a very sad indicator of the decline of a culture. I recently saw a Cheyenne quote on a website that said, "A Nation is not conquered until the hearts of its women are on the ground, then it is done. No matter how brave its warriors or how strong its weapons." Perhaps the same could be said about the nation's Elders. When the Elders are left out of the vital loop of life, no longer charged with the challenge of contributing their wisdom, understanding, and knowledge to the younger generations . . . they simply get old and our culture declines as a result of it.

In some early tribal cultures, the task of surviving from one day to the next was so arduous that the younger members of the tribe, those of childbearing age, were expected to provide for the food and safety needs of the others. The grandparents and older aunts and uncles were the primary daily caregivers of the little ones. It was also recognized that these more experienced members of the tribe had both more patience and more wisdom to give to the children. The circle of the family rippled out around the children in a sphere of care and influence. In Lakota country, this extended family is called the *tiyospaye*.

In many of the modern Indian communities we visited this is still very much the general practice. Sadly, there are also a huge number of little ones in the care of grandparents because the parents got caught in the deadly web of alcohol, gambling, or violence. This is true not only in Indian country but in all communities. When the grandparent takes the *full role* of parent, they lose their place as grandparent and Elder.

This topic, the erosion of the Elder status within families and communities, certainly deserves its own deep exploration as it echoes through the generations. Like our youth, the Elders have increasingly become a target of the drug companies. Recently a friend's mother was in psychiatric care for depression. Over several months her medications were switched, rotated, and stacked one upon the other until the poor woman finally went into a toxic overdose. She ended up in a coma in the hospital. Many Elders are under the care of multiple doctors with several medications being prescribed and no one overseeing the entire regime.

Like youth, our Elders need challenge. John Ratey (2001)[1] in *A User's Guide to the Brain*, wrote about an interesting research project done by David Snowdon, a University of Kentucky professor. He studied a group of nuns living in a monastery in Mankato, Minnesota who were living into their late nineties and early hundreds with strong minds and bodies. Snowdon wanted to know why. He discovered that the nuns, operating on the belief that "an idle mind is the devil's plaything," had numerous weekly programs intended to stimulate the mind. They held reading groups and debates, brought in speakers, wrote in their journals, and had study sessions. Ratey (2001) wrote,

> "Snowdon, who has examined more than 100 brains donated at death by nuns in Mankato and other School Sisters locations across the nation, maintains that the axons and dendrites that usually shrink with age branch out and make new connections if there is enough intellectual stimulation, providing a bigger backup system if some pathways fail."

It appears that the brain, like a muscle, atrophies without active use. If we shuffle our Elder parents and grandparents off to the side, limiting their involvement in our lives, the effects on their health and brain functioning can be disastrous.

This poses a great challenge to our culture. Our families are scattered like leaves in autumn. Even in my own life, my grandchildren live ten hours away. It is painful for me to not be available to assist my daughters during these early years of their marriage when they are in college or having babies and still trying to find their way in the world. My place is near them. I feel that in my bones—and the telephone is a very poor substitute. As I've worked on this book over the past several years, it's become clearer to me that to create a true Elder-based culture, families need to stick together. Holidays twice a year simply don't cut it.

In this new millennium, the Elders are living longer, living alone, and often living far from their families. We have this strange belief that when we finally get the kids out of the house, it's our turn to play. Just as our culture is rife with social assumptions about our clueless kids, we have social assumptions that the relatives should butt out of the lives of our young ones. Strange. Like the missing rituals for adolescent rites of passage, it occurs to me that I have no clue what an Elder-based culture would really look like.

We operate under a notion of independence that makes no sense and serves us poorly. We act as if we don't (or shouldn't) need each other, and then wonder why we feel isolated and alone. However, creating this Elder connection is not the same as the undeveloped adult running home to have mom and dad take care of life for them. Except for a few very close-knit and small native communities I've visited, I have no model in the current culture to draw on.

During one of our collection trips to southeast Alaska, we met a Tlingit woman named Marge. Marge was probably in her early sixties, a beautiful and vibrant woman. As we talked with her, she told us that she was being prepared and initiated by her Elders to become an Elder herself. Marge was not taking this action lightly. Being an Elder in her community, she explained, was a true commitment and responsibility that is not simply given but must be earned. As I listened to her, I realized that, rather like the president of the United States, the fate of the younger generations rested on her ability to make wise and careful choices. In Lakota country, people are taught to consider their decisions based on how that decision would affect the next seven generations.

As we've seen through these discussions on levels of development and the maturing brain, we don't automatically get wise when we get old. We must strive for it. To become an Elder we must also be initiated into that status.

On our final night in southeast Alaska, we had supper with Marge at her house. After a wonderful meal of freshly caught halibut, Marge explained that she would like to perform a song and dance in honor of our visit. She put on her own mother's button blanket, took up an eagle feather, and did a slow-moving dance in her living room while she sang. Her sincere offering touched my soul deeply. I'd lost my mother just six months earlier to illness and was still grieving her loss. Something about Marge and her slow movements evoked that grief within me. When she finished her dance, I started to cry. I was a little embarrassed but the tears were beyond my control. Marge was very sweet and comforted me.

When I woke up in the hotel room the next morning, my lower back went into spasms. The pain was incredible. I found a chiropractor and a massage therapist, but the spasms only worsened. Thankfully, we were at the end of the trip, and I crabbed my way across airports and parking lots and finally made it home. I was completely taken over by my pain. For the next two weeks I couldn't seem to do anything to relieve the spasms.

Finally, one night I was explaining to Milt that I couldn't understand why I was feeling so sad—for no reason. He gently reminded me that my mother had just died—and that perhaps my experience with Marge and my mother's death were related. His words tapped a deep pool of grief, and I started to cry again. I cried for hours, even crying myself to sleep that night.

I missed my Mom. I wanted her back again in physical form, back in her chair in her little house working crossword puzzles and waiting for me to call. When Marge wore her mother's blanket across her shoulders, sheltered and warm, I think my soul began to cry out for that. After crying the night through, I woke up the next morning and the back pain had completely disappeared.

Hellinger says we need the strength of our ancestors and our parents behind us—at our backs—if we are to stand strong in the world. I once heard him speak about low back pain sometimes resulting from not taking the support of the parents and ancestors. When we don't feel supported, or are unwilling to take that support, it makes us weak. Honoring the Elders is not just a social nicety that says we should honor them. No, it is a deep need to have them *back us up* and make us strong.

In my work as a facilitator of family constellations, one picture I find particularly beautiful is to see a woman or a man with seven generations of parents and grandparents at his or her back. When we stand in this place, we see that our generation is just a small foothill in the great mountain range of our ancestors. We feel their strength.

One of the Ten Commandments of the Jewish and Christian religions is to "Honor Thy Father and Mother." Too often this commandment is taken as a social rule or courtesy (not deeply felt) that we extend to our parents out of respect. My understanding of this has changed with the study of Hellinger's work. We honor our parents not for their benefit—but for our own. Our strength in the world comes from the two portals of our parents from which life flowed through to us. We need our Elders—they do not need us.

In many tribal and other cultures around the world, the spirits of the ancestors are treated as real entities that exist and surround us. The Elders take their guidance from this direction in prayer and ceremony, beseeching the spirits to assist them. The true genius and pioneering courage of Hellinger's work has been in his willingness to consider that the influence of the ancestors and past generations can extend beyond the grave into the present generations. In some religious and scientific circles, this is a cause of uneasiness.

This discussion, while seeming to stray off into the Mysteries, is of particular importance for if we are to define an Elder-based culture. Each member of a system must seek guidance from the ones behind him or her. To the three-year-old, an older brother of ten is an Elder. To a twenty-year-old, the parents or grandparents are the Elders. If you are eighty, your Elders may be in the spirit world. The stairway to heaven is generational—and only those on a higher treads can show us the way.

The deeper structures of the family system are like a giant reservoir far upstream, the larger body of energy that Hellinger chooses to call simply "the greater force." The ancestral line and the two parents who give life are like the place in the dam where the water is released and allowed to begin its flow downstream.

The river of life is a river of love. It flows down to us from above. Without our Elders we, quite simply, wouldn't exist.

Conclusion

Before writing this book, before Hellinger, even before my children became adolescents, I had a vision. It came to me after listening to an ancient Lakota story about *Makah*, Mother Earth (mother of all), and the second cleansing of the earth. In the ancient story, *Makah* has become displeased with the people. They war and fight, take no care of her living body, and no longer listen to the Elders. Makah, in her displeasure, brings only a few of the people deep within her body and then ruthlessly shakes the rest of the people off the planet. This event, the story says, is called the "second cleansing." Later, those who were taken inside re-emerged from her belly as the Lakota people and, once again, began populating the planet.

When I first heard this story from a Lakota Elder many years ago, I began to think that Makah must certainly be frustrated once again with her angry, unaware, warring children. Perhaps she prepares to do a third and final cleansing. What, if anything, would keep her from shaking us off once again, I wondered?

The answer? Love. Only love. Massive amounts of love could convince her that we were worthy of living on her beautiful body. Love for each other, love for the earth, love for all other creatures. Love.

I began writing a story with the main plot constructed around a revolution of love happening on planet earth. In my story, Makah is disgusted and displeased, ready to toss us off again when, unexpectedly, her sweet granddaughter asks for the opportunity to give the people one more chance to prove their ability to love. Makah agrees to let her try and sends her granddaughter down among the people in a human body.

I put the awakening scene in the beautiful Badlands of South Dakota because it seemed that here, for sure, magic could happen. Then I sent two small Lakota boys to discover the strange woman asleep under an embankment. Next I saw the spirits flying in like racing storm clouds from all corners of the earth to assist Makah's granddaughter in bringing about this revolution of the heart.

At this point, I fell deeply in love with my own story which I titled *One Drum*. Its characters were people just like me trying to find the Good Road, but not always succeeding. I loved the image of the Ancestors and the Great Beings all arriving, unseen and invisible, to help save us from our own foolish selves. In a final scene, the two boys gather around a drum at the base of Bear Butte, a sacred mountain, to drum the new rhythm for all time. They are surrounded and assisted by these Great Beings.

Today, as I read this beautiful story again, I see it not as fiction but perhaps as reality. My sight has grown keen. I see those wise ones all around waiting only for us to humbly ask, "Please help us." An invisible hand is at work in the world; it guides this purple pen as I write, it inspires the amazing works of scholars like Senge, Fritz, Pearce, LeShan, and others. I see it at work blurring the lines and boundaries between scientific study and spiritual pursuit, creating the crossover pioneers like Hellinger, Erickson, Bohm, Dossey, and many others. It is a revolution of the heart.

To all of these invisible beings, I ask humbly and directly, "Please help us to fashion a culture that supports its little ones, that reveres its old ones, and cares deeply for Mother Earth." Our culture seeks a deeper solution than our task forces and small problem-solving armies can provide. We need the special language of the heart, embedded in story and ritual that only the heart speaks. Help is all around if we only ask.

On the day I wrote these final paragraphs, I had a phone call from a man in Iowa who heard one of our *Oyate* programs on the radio. Actually, he had heard the show a while ago, scribbled the number down on an old receipt, and then stuffed the slip into his glove box. When he called our 800 number, he couldn't recall why he had written the number down so he opened the conversation by asking me, "Do you know what you do?"

Of course, some days I ask myself the same question, so I laughed and said, "Yes, I think so." As soon as I told him about the *Oyate* series, he immediately remembered hearing the program. He told me that when it began he had to pull into a parking lot to listen. Then he said something like, "I heard your heart in that program."

His words touched something in me and, instead of taking an order, I found myself telling him about constellation work, kids and culture, this book—I even told him my astrological sign. We had an animated conversation that lasted nearly forty-five minutes. He agreed to help spread this work across the country.

What I didn't tell him was that the night before I had asked all those unseen beings to help me with this work, to find the right people who can find the right people who will make a revolution of love. And then, a stranger was calling me from nowhere!

Let's find each other, you speakers of the language of the heart who are out there reading books, praying, talking to the spirits, and raising your children to be awake and aware. Let's put our heads together, our hearts together, and make our families and culture strong once again. This is no time for sitting on fences, walking the middle road, or keeping your truest thoughts to yourself.

The next time a little girl falls in the hot sun, let's catch her quick, before she falls.

Chapter Endnotes

Introduction

1. Gina Score's tragic experience ended in the closing of the state boot camp at Plankinton. Reports on this event can be found at several sites on the Internet by simply entering her name.

2. Ritalin statistic taken from a paper presented by Peter Breggins before the Subcommittee on Oversight and Investigations Committee and the Workforce, U.S. House of Representatives. Peter Breggins is a strong voice in the controversy against the massive use of legal, psychotropic drugs for children. I recommend the reader examine his books (listed in the reference section) concerning this issue or visit his website at www.breggin.com

3. Suicide and adolescence. This information is provided by the American Association of Suicidology in Washington, D.C. You can visit their website at www.suicidology.org. Their fact sheet says that suicide ranks as the third leading cause of death for young people between the ages of 15 and 29. Suicide rates for ages 15-19 are 300% higher than those of the 1950's.

4. 200,000 youth incarcerated. For further information and statistics on the incarceration rates of youth and the juvenile justice system in the U.S. visit www.restorativejustice.org. This site is also a font of information on alternatives to incarceration. I've only just recently gotten involved with our local Restorative Justice organization but I'm very impressed at their commitment and dedication to this issue. Check out this site.

5. Bert Hellinger: I discovered the work of Bert Hellinger, a German psychotherapist, in the spring of 1998 during a demonstration of this work by another German, Heinz Stark. Hellinger works with energetic fields within a family or relationship system. Hellinger acknowledges Milton Erickson, Fritz Perls, Arthur Janov, Neurolinguistic Programming (NLP) and others as key influences on his work. It is my thinking that Hellinger's work extends these early movements in a powerful and profound way. In the fall of 2002 we traveled to Austria to interview Hellinger for a documentary program on this work. The CD of this interview, On Love and Other Things, A Conversation with Bert Hellinger, is available for purchase at

www.manykites.com. Additional articles, calendar of events and information on Hellinger can be found on his website at www.hiddensymetry.com.

6. Oyate Ta Olowan—Songs of the People: This was a public radio series produced by my husband, Milt, and me during the period 1995-2000. The series has 52 half-hour programs featuring Native American musicians from across the continent and several islands, including American Samoa and Hawaii. Two of the programs have received Golden Reel Awards from the National Federation of Community Broadcasters. Funding for the series was provided by The Corporation for Public Broadcasting and the National Endowment for the Arts. To read more about the Oyate series, visit www.oyate.com.

Chapter One

1. Apache Sunrise Ceremony: We attended this ceremony in the company of a medicine man, Harris Burnette, who was also one of the singers we interviewed for Oyate Ta Olowan. Harris was one of the traditional men that we met that would only agree to be interviewed after doing a ceremony and requesting the permission of the spirits. Harris agreed to be recorded in the hopes that his songs would aid in the healing of the planet and its inhabitants. You can hear a sample of his singing on www.oyate.com.

2. Michael Ventura, The Utne Reader (July, 1994) under the title "Today's Teens, Dissed, Mythed and Totally Pissed. This provocative set of articles set me off on the trail of further research into the question of youth in our current culture. The article referred to several writers on the topic including Malidoma Some, Luis J. Rodriguez, Sara Ferguson, Andrea N. Jones and Douglas Foster.

3. The Hupa Tribe is actually a grouping of seven different coastal tribes that were forced together into one tribe by the U.S. government. Their beautiful village, Hoopa, California, rests along a valley bottom along the Trinity River.

Chapter Two

1. Some', Malidoma Patrice. (1993). Ritual: Power, Healing and Community. Swan/Raven and Co. Malidoma Some' has written and taught extensively on the use of ritual in

daily life as a means of connecting ourselves with the power of the spirit and soul. I have not heard him speak personally but have met others who speak highly of his work. I first encountered his work in the same Utne Reader article on adolescence in which I encountered Michael Ventura.

2. Unangax People. Ethan Pettigrew, our host during this collection trip, was very specific in saying that the people of his tribe prefer their own name, Unangax, rather than Aleut, the name given them by invaders. This tiny island has quite a tale to tell in the deceptive moves by the U.S. military in removing all the inhabitants of the island during World War Two. The Unangax people were taken to southeast Alaska and kept in an old cannery. Many died and the struggle to return home was immense.

3. Frank Furstenberg (2000) "The sociology of adolescence and youth in the 1990s: A critical commentary." Journal of Marriage and the Family; (Minneapolis; Nov 2000). This was an informative and interesting article that I stumbled across in a literature search. I had not really thought of the idea that the adolescent "stage" had been created by our society with the introduction of mandatory education to age sixteen.

Chapter Three

1. Silverman, Linda and Shupin, Elizabeth. (1981) "Crises and the higher development of women." A paper presented at the American Psychological Association's annual convention in Los Angeles, CA. This article came to me from a friend of mine who had gone to a treatment center in Colorado for Multiple Sclerosis. She handed me the article and I was immediately struck by how it matched my experience at the time. I was consciously seeking a wider experience of my life, but felt deeply frustrated with the limits and rules that seemed to be confining me. I followed their references into the work of Kazmierez Dabrowski and the theory of positive disintegration.

2. Kazmierez Dabrowski. It is difficult to locate copies of Dabrowski's books but there is a good website maintained by Bill Tiller that is dedicated to Dabrowski's work http://members.shaw.ca/positivedisintegration/ This information, interestingly, has become a framework for working with gifted children who are "overexcitable." This term, coined by

Dabrowski, describes an important aspect of our development as humans.

3. LeShan, Lawrence. (1992). The psychology of war: Comprehending its mystique and its mystery. Chicago: The Noble Press, Inc. I took this book off the shelf of my local library and was amazed that it was sitting on the car seat next to me on September 11 when the shocking events of the collapsing Trade Towers and the imminent possibility of war suddenly hit. I had to read it. I found myself reading words describing ideas that I could look up at the television screen and see unfold in front of me. I watched our American people mobilize in what LeShan calls the mythic reality of good versus evil and a justified war. His thinking fascinates me.

After laying some groundwork, LeShan describes how humans are able to move from a sensory reality to a mythic reality around war. He explores what he calls the "tension" all human beings experience between being individual and being part of or belonging to a group. He explains that if we want to understand why war is so popular (even in the face of potential total destruction of the race) we must understand this tension within human nature. When humans have collected in the mythic reality of right equals might, we are very sure of ourselves, very together, very committed. This, in simple terms, feels good.

Interestingly, LeShan says that there are only two ways to relieve the tension between our aloneness and our need to belong. One is to follow a spiritual discipline to a higher level of thinking and the other is war. I strongly recommend this book to all readers interested in a world filled with peace.

Chapter Four

1. The Humblecha is a Lakota ceremony known as the vision quest. It is not specifically a rites of passage ceremony. Rather, it has the purpose of assisting the individual in finding the guiding vision of his or her life. The ceremony lasts several days and includes fasting, cleansing, praying and spending time alone on the mountain.

2. Nave, Ari. "Rites of Passage and Transition." http://www.africana.com/Articles/tt_466.htm Okiek People of Kenya. This is an African rite of passage ritual that exists for both boys and girls.

3. Carlos Castaneda. (1968). The Teaching of Don Juan: a Yaqui way of knowledge. New York: Ballantine Books. This book was an important part of my own initiatory years during early college. I followed Castaneda through his important journey.

4. Robert Fritz has created a model for understanding the creative process in terms of structural tension systems. He is the author of The Path of Least Resistance and several other books exploring the creative process. I was fortunate enough to do a couple of seminars with Robert and his wife, Rosalind, and their work is impressive and worth examining.

5. Senge, P. (2000). Schools that learn. New York: Doubleday. This book, along with Senge's earlier book, The Fifth Discipline, provides a marvelous set of resources on how to become a learning society. I'm expecting to have a romance with this material over the next several years and to become fluent with the ideas contained within it.

Chapter Five

1. Smilkstein, Rita. We're Born to Learn, Corwin Press. While I was teaching at Oglala Lakota College I began to use an out-of-print textbook called Tools for Writing that was written by Rita. She has spent much of her career asking the question "How do people learn naturally?" Over time she developed an approach which she called The Natural Human Learning Process (NHLP) that is based on how the brain naturally builds neural networks when engaged in the right way. The result of using her textbook with my uncertain students was astounding. My retention jumped to 80 percent and my students seemed to love learning grammar. All educators should read Rita's book and begin to model this approach. Learning should be fun and exciting. How have we gotten so far off base?

Chapter Six

1. Stark, Heinz. Heinz was my first trainer in the Family Constellation Work. He was also one of the first to bring this work to the United States. During one of his first trips to South Dakota, Milt and I took him out to the Pine Ridge Reservation and put him on KILI FM radio to do an interview on the work. We also impulsively arranged a demonstration of

the work that night in Kyle. 25 people showed up this led to bringing him back to the reservation for multiple workshops. Our publishing house, Many Kites Press, also published a collection of his essays entitled Systemic Constellation Work as Art. You may want to check it out.

2. Senge, Peter. The Fifth Discipline. I highly recommend this book to any who would like to better understand the workings of social and business groups.

3. Breggins, Peter. Talking Back to Prozac. Also highly recommended—but frightening. Breggins is a strong spokesman against the overuse of psychotropic drugs in the treatment of human growth issues. I highly recommend Talking Back to Prozac and his other books to any seeking to better understand the threat posed to us by an industry too dedicated to profit and not to human development.

4. Pearce, J. Chilton. (1992). Evolution's end. San Francisco: Harper Collins. I have read most of Pearce's other works and was excited about finding this book. Pearce has been instrumental in my own thinking about human development and even how I act with my own children. Evolution's End is a fascinating suggestion to us that the sum total of brain development and human behavior is to activate the brain to become a "receiver" and not just a "processor." His belief is that the neo-cortex, when highly developed and carefully tended, is capable of receiving information from larger sources of knowledge and information that he humorously calls "soup sources." The suggestion is that the information exists outside of the human brain in nonlocal reality and that the brain is designed to extend outside of the body to receive this information. This receiver function explains much of what has been previously called the "paranormal." Synchronicity, collective unconscious, intuition, clairvoyance, and the mysterious "knowing" that we sometimes have come from these external "soup sources." He also explains that we both draw from and contribute to these collective bodies of knowledge in a co-creative way. Pearce says that this is the developmental goal of evolution itself.

Chapters Seven-through Ten

These chapters are all based on my own experience as a writer. However, I can share my favorite "getting in touch

172

with yourself" books for writers. Check out Writing Down the Bones and Wild Mind by Natalie Goldberg, The Artist's Way by Julia Cameron, and Bird by Bird by Anne Lamott. All of these books will help you mine the gold in your inner self.

Chapter Eleven

1. John Ratey's book, A User's Guide to the Brain, is a wonderful basic book on the brain. A person new to the study of the brain can quickly become overwhelmed by the research and conflicting data available. This book is easy to read and gives a good summary of current theories on the brain.

Bibliography

Avila, Elena. (2000). Woman who glows in the dark: a Curandera reveals Aztec secrets of physical and spiritual health. NY: Putnam Publishing Group.

Baldwin, Christina. (1994). Calling the circle: the first and future culture. North Carolina: Swan Raven and Co.

Block, Peter. (1993). Stewardship: Choosing service over self-interest. San Francisco: Berrett-Koehler Publishers, Inc.

Bly, Robert. (1996). The Sibling Society. Reading, Massachusetts: Addison-Wesley Publishing Company.

Breggins, Peter. (1990). Talking back to Prozac: What doctors aren't telling you about today's most controversial drug. New York: St. Martin's Press.

Breggins, Peter. (2000). Testimony Before the Subcommittee on Oversight and Investigations Committee on Education and the Workforce, U.S. House of Representatives.[Online]. Available: [httl://www.breggin.com.htm add internet address]

Breggins, Peter. & Cohen, D. (1999). Your drugs may be your problem. Cambridge, MA: Perseus Publishing.

Castenada, Carlos. (1968). Teachings of Don Juan: a Yaqui way of knowledge. New York: Ballantine Books.

Chappel, Tom. (1993). The soul of a business: Managing for profit and the common good. New York: Bantam Books.

Dabrowski, Kazimierz. (1964). Positive disintegration. Boston: Little Brown and Co.

Dabrowski, Kazimierz. (1972). Psychoneuroses is not an illness. London: Gryf Publications.

Frank Furstenberg (2000). "The sociology of adolescence and youth in the 1990s: A critical commentary." Journal of Marriage and the Family; Minneapolis.

Garnett, L. R. (2000, May 7). Prozac revisited. The Boston Globe, p. A01.

Glenmullen, J. (2000). Prozac backlash: Overcoming the dangers of Prozac, Zoloft, Paxil and other antidepressants with safe, effective alternatives. New York: Simon and Schuster.

Hellinger, Bert. (1998). Love's hidden symmetry. Phoenix: Zeig Tucker and Co.

Hellinger, Bert. (2001). Love's own truths. Phoenix: Zeig Tucker and Co.

LeShan, Lawrence. (1992). The psychology of war: Comprehending its mystique and its mystery. Chicago: The Noble Press, Inc.

Meade, Michael. (1993). Men and the water of life: Initiation and the tempering of men. San Francisco: HarperSanFran.

MacLean, P. D. (1975.) A mind of three minds: Educating the triune brain. Offprint from the Seventy-seventh Yearbook of the National Society for the Study of Education. Chicago.

Pearce, J.Chilton. (1986). Magical child. New York: Bantam.

Pearce, J. Chilton. (1992). Evolution's end. San Francisco: Harper Collins.

Piaget, Jean. (1970). Science of education and the psychology of the child. New York: Orion Press.

Ratey, John. (2001). A user's guide to the brain. New York: Pantheon Books.

Senge, Peter. (1990). Fifth discipline. New York: Doubleday.

Senge, P. (2000). Schools that learn. New York: Doubleday.

Sheldrake, Rupert. (1995). Seven experiments that could change the world: A do-it yourself guide to revolutionary science. New York: River Books.

Silverman, Linda and Shupin, Elizabeth. "Crises and the higher development of women." Paper presented at the American Psychological Association Annual Convention, Los Angeles, 1981.

Some', Malidoma Patrice. (1993). Ritual; power healing and community. North Carolina: Swan/Raven and Co.

Some', Malidoma Patrice. (1994, July) "Today's Teens, Dissed, Mythed and Totally Pissed." Utne Reader, 64:50-67.

Ventura, Michael. (1993). Letters at 3 AM: Reports on endarkment. Spring Publications.

Ventura, Michael. (1994, July). "Today's Teens, Dissed, Mythed and Totally Pissed" Utne Reader, 64:50-67.

About the Author

Patricia "Jamie" Lee has traveled extensively into Indian Country with her husband, Milt Lee, an enrolled member of the Cheyenne River Sioux Tribe. Together they have produced over seventy public radio documentaries including the 52-part native series, *Oyate Ta Olowan—The Songs of the People.* Their work has aired internationally and received six Golden Reel Awards from the National Federation of Community Broadcasters with major funding from The Corporation for Public Broadcasting and The National Endowment for the Arts.

In 2007 Lee's first novel, *Washaka—The Bear Dreamer,* was a finalist in the PEN USA Literary Awards. Her short fiction has been published in *The South Dakota Review, Winds of Change Magazine, Heartlands Magazine, Byline* and others, and in 2006 she received a South Dakota Arts Council grant for fiction.

Lee has an MA in Human Development and was a developmental English instructor at Oglala Lakota College on The Pine Ridge Reservation for five years. She grew up on The Leech Lake Reservation in northern Minnesota. Jamie and her husband are currently building a straw bale home on ten acres in her home territory.

A Final Note from the Author

This book is already nearly two decades old. I was young when I wrote it, and now I advance toward becoming an Elder myself. In this new addition, several chapters have been removed because they have since become either full books or resources. One chapter fully outlined the five levels of spiritual development. Another focused on the Family Constellation Work of Bert Hellinger.

The constellation chapter is now a full handbook filled with exercises you can do to strengthen yourself and your family. The Taming Power of Love will be available by June of 2010.

Also, since the first edition of this book, we have begun a nation-wide outreach initiative called *The Strong Family Project*. This project began with the release of our film, *Video Letters from Prison* in the summer of 2010. There are many ways for you to become involved with these projects or to share your own stories, so please browse our website to access some of these resources.

www.manykites.org
books, film clips, etc.

www.jamielee.manykites.org
Patricia Jamie Lee's blog

videolettersfromprison.org
Strong Family activities and how to
set up a screening/workshop in your area

www.ingramcontent.com/pod-product-compliance
Lightning Source LLC
LaVergne TN
LVHW051121080426
835510LV00018B/2155